SCIENCE FIX

DANNY NICHOLSON

SCIENCE FIX

SCIENCE MADE EASY FOR PRIMARY TEACHERS

CORWIN

A SAGE Publishing Company

1 Oliver's Yard
55 City Road
London EC1Y 1SP

2455 Teller Road
Thousand Oaks
California 91320

Unit No 323-333, Third Floor, F-Block
International Trade Tower
Nehru Place, New Delhi – 110 019

8 Marina View Suite 43-053
Asia Square Tower 1
Singapore 018960

Editor: Amy Thornton
Senior project editor: Chris Marke
Cover design: Wendy Scott
Typeset by: C&M Digitals (P) Ltd, Chennai, India

Library of Congress Control Number: 2024935910

British Library Cataloguing in Publication data

A catalogue record for this book is available from the
British Library

ISBN 978-1-0719-2861-5
ISBN 978-1-0719-2860-8 (pbk)

Dedication

To my daughter, Amelia. Never stop asking questions. Stay curious!

Contents

Acknowledgements

I would like to thank the staff and students of:

Billericay Educational Consortium (now NESTT)
Essex and Thames SCITT
Pilgrim Partnership SCITT

for their help, support and encouragement over the years.
Thanks to Angie McGlashon for getting me involved in SCITT training in the first place.
And special thanks to my wife Sarah for her constant support and for putting up with a garage crammed with plastic crates full of science stuff.

Image acknowledgements

The following images are reproduced (with permission) from Roden and Archer, *Primary Science for Trainee Teachers* (2014), Learning Matters: London.

Figure 4.1 The parts of a flower (Roden and Archer, p. 33)
Figure 5.1 Invertebrates: animals without backbones (Roden and Archer, p. 89)
Figure 6.1 The digestive system (Roden and Archer, p. 52)
Figure 9.1 Domains in a magnetic material before and after magnetisation (Roden and Archer, p. 139)
Figure 9.2 Forces acting on an object (Roden and Archer, p. 142)

The following images are reproduced (with permission) from Peacock et al., *Primary Science Knowledge and Understanding*, 9th edn (2021), Learning Matters: London.

Figure 10.1 Day and night (June) (Peacock et al., p. 287)
Figure 10.2 The seasons (Peacock at al., p. 289)
Figure 10.3 The phases of the Moon (Peacock at al., p. 291)
Figure 12.1 The human eye (Peacock at al., p. 247)

About the author

Danny Nicholson is a Science and Computing lecturer for Billericay Educational Consortium and Essex and Thames Primary SCITT on their Primary SCITT teacher training courses. He also works as an independent trainer, author and consultant. He is the author of *Reach Out CPD* and co-wrote schemes such as Switched on Science for KS2 and Eureka: Success in Science for KS3.

About this book

Many primary school teachers find science a difficult subject to teach. Not only do teachers need to develop their own knowledge of a complex subject, but they also need to know how to bring this subject to life in the primary classroom. In their 2023 Science report, Ofsted highlighted that very few schools have a clear plan to develop teachers' knowledge of science and how to teach it through CPD (Ofsted 2023). *Science Fix* is here to help. It supports teachers to develop their knowledge of science and how to teach it.

Science Fix is an introduction to the effective teaching of primary science for teachers and trainee teachers. It provides a breakdown of the complete primary science curriculum and outlines the science knowledge needed to teach each area. It includes practical advice for planning and delivering sequences of science lessons. The focus is on ensuring lessons are engaging and educational. Throughout the book, I have included a range of practical activities and demonstrations that can be used to engage primary school pupils and promote scientific thinking. I have also identified common misconceptions that children may have about science.

In writing this book, I have drawn on my many years of experience supporting new primary science teachers.

Bonus online content

Bonus content can be found on my website at: www.sciencefix.co.uk/bonus

PART 1

CHAPTER 1

What is Science and Why Do We Teach It?

Introduction

I have been involved in primary teacher education for nearly 20 years, first as a science lecturer, then also as a computing lecturer. Whenever I talk to primary student teachers in those early weeks of their SCITT course, so many of them tell me how much they hated science when they were at school, usually their secondary school experience, and in particular their GCSE courses. This is a shame, as quite often they turned against science because of how the subject was taught, the amount of content or the high-stakes approach in KS4.

When I press them on their experiences in primary schools, the memories of some of the things they did during lessons start to come back. They can remember growing cress, looking for minibeasts, making circuits. They remember the practical things they did in science, and they remember it fondly. Very few recall writing things down or completing a worksheet.

Science is an experiential subject – there are lots of things to make and do, and it's those things that stick in the memory. And here's the thing: primary science is great. There are many wonderful topics you can cover, and it really gives you a chance to inspire a feeling of awe and wonder in children about the world around them.

Very few of the students in an average primary SCITT (School Centred Initial Teacher Training) cohort will have an A-level in a science subject and, if they do, then it is probably in biology. GCSE science classes would be the last time they did any science, which may have been a long time ago, particularly for students who have spent time in the world of work before deciding to become a teacher. Successful science teachers need to have great science subject knowledge and understanding (SKU) and also an understanding of the theories behind how to teach science to primary age children. I hope that in the course of my teaching, I can rekindle a love for science in others.

So, these are the aims of this book: to sell the joys of science and science teaching, and to help you become a great primary science teacher.

Why teach science?

Pupils should be inspired by their first formal educational encounters with science at primary school (Wellcome, 2014). Primary science should develop pupils' understanding of the world, nurture their curiosity and teach essential skills, including enquiry, observation, prediction, analysis, reasoning and explanation.

The aims of the national curriculum for science are to develop pupils'

- scientific knowledge and understanding of the natural and physical world;
- scientific skills and processes;
- scientific attitudes and values;
- scientific literacy and citizenship.

Knowledge in science

The science knowledge that is taught in schools can be considered to be two separate types:

Substantive knowledge This is the knowledge of the scientific concepts, such as the names of planets, parts of a flower or the bones in the body. This is often referred to as 'scientific knowledge'.

Disciplinary knowledge This is the knowledge of how scientific knowledge is generated. In principle, this is the working scientifically or 'doing science' strand of the curriculum and includes how to carry out practical activities.

If presented with an image of a leaf insect, what knowledge would you need to decide whether it was a plant or an animal? You would need the substantive knowledge of the features of plants and animals. You would also need disciplinary knowledge about classification. If substantive knowledge is the stuff that we know, disciplinary knowledge is the understanding of how we found out that stuff.

The scientific method

At a very basic level, science is about being inquisitive and asking 'why?'. The role of science is to explain the world around us as best we can, using all available evidence.

The scientific method can be traced back to Ibn al-Haytham, the Arab scholar, around the turn of the eleventh century, who applied it to his study of optics and astronomy. His ideas were later adopted by Renaissance scholars such as Galileo.

The scientific method of thinking starts with a question – for example, 'Why does something happen the way it does?' This might lead to a prediction of what might happen. An experiment could then be carried out, in which this prediction is tested and evidence is collected. A judgement is then made as to whether the evidence is strong enough to support or reject the prediction. This in turn might generate new questions which can also be tested. Sadly, in the reality of the classroom, there is often not enough time to investigate these new questions.

In the primary classroom, the process could look like that shown in Figure 1.1.

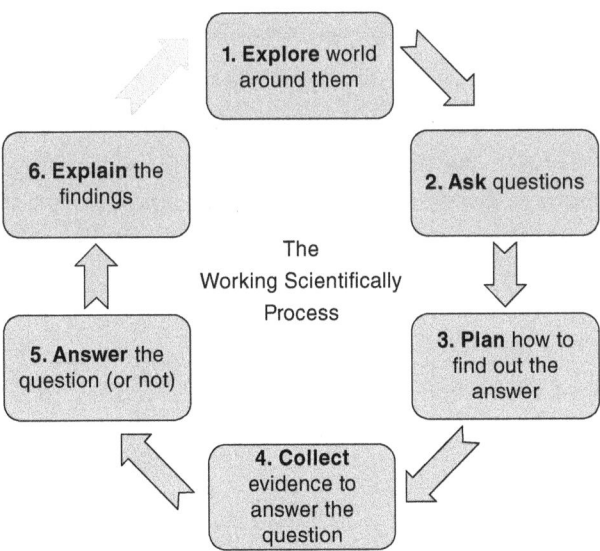

Figure 1.1   The working scientifically process

Scientific enquiry or working scientifically describes the processes and skills that pupils should be taught and use to find out more about the world and how it works (ASE, 2018). This will be looked at in more detail in Chapter 2.

Do scientists know everything?

It might seem that science has an answer for everything, but there's still a lot that isn't known and even the things that we do know are not always completely understood.

Scientists build models to explain phenomena based on the best evidence available at the time. If new evidence can be found that suggests something different, and that evidence can be backed up and checked by others, then even long-held ideas can be updated and amended. By comparison, the internet conspiracy theorists will stick to their stories despite the evidence to the contrary.

Science adjusts its views based on what's observed.

Faith is the denial of observation so that Belief can be preserved

Listen to the whole of Tim Minchin's poem 'Storm', which perfectly sums up the battle that rational thinkers have against the tide of alternative facts (Minchin, 2009).

What is a theory?

A theory means something different to scientists than it does to everyone else. In everyday usage, a theory means a guess or a hunch, and these theories are often unproven. In science, a theory is a well-accepted explanation for a phenomenon based on the best evidence available. A theory ties together all the facts and can be used to make predictions that can be tested. In science, a theory is as close to proven as it is possible to be with the evidence available at the time. Gravity may be a 'theory' but are you prepared to test it by jumping out of a window? Other famous theories that are familiar include Einstein's Theory of Relativity, Darwin's Theory of Evolution by Natural Selection, and many more.

The big ideas in science

So, what are the big ideas that underpin the science curriculum? What are the important concepts we need to cover?

Harlen (2010) compiled a list of scientific principles that underpin the science knowledge of all pupils throughout their time in school. A broad understanding of science concepts is important to have a scientifically literate population of adults.

According to Harlen (2010), there are ten big ideas *of* science:

1. All material in the universe is made of very small particles.
2. Objects can affect other objects at a distance.
3. Changing the movement of an object requires a net force to be acting on it.
4. The total amount of energy in the universe is always the same, but energy can be transformed when things change or are made to happen.
5. The composition of the earth and its atmosphere and the processes occurring within them shape the earth's surface and its climate.
6. The solar system is a very small part of one of millions of galaxies in the universe.
7. Organisms are organised on a cellular basis.
8. Organisms require a supply of energy and materials for which they are often dependent or in competition with other organisms.
9. Genetic information is passed down from one generation of organisms to another.
10. The diversity of organisms, living and extinct, is the result of evolution.

There are four big ideas *about* science:

1. Science assumes that for every effect there is one or more causes.
2. Scientific explanations, theories and models are those that best fit the facts known at a particular time.
3. The knowledge produced by science is used in some technologies to create products to serve human ends.
4. Applications of science often have ethical, social, economic and political implications.

Nearly all of these ideas are introduced in the primary national curriculum with the exception of energy transformations. This can be quite an abstract concept for younger children, and it is not introduced until Key Stage 3 when pupils can best understand energy stores and energy transfers. In primary science, it is best to use physical processes and mechanisms, rather than energy, to explain and investigate phenomena (Tracy, 2014).

Constructivism and misconceptions

Pupils do not come into school as an empty vessel, ready to be filled with science knowledge; rather, they come with their own sets of ideas and concepts that they will have built to explain how the world around them works. This is a *constructivist* view of learning, drawing on the work of psychologists such as Piaget and Vygotsky. Leinhardt (1992) stated that the essence of *constructivist* theory is the idea that learners must individually discover and transform complex information if they are to make it their own.

A **misconception** can be defined as a view that does not fully coincide with the scientific view. Often these existing ideas are produced through informal play or through watching films and television shows. These ideas are at odds with the accepted science and they can be difficult to change or reform, and become a source of misconceptions when met in formal science lessons (Allen, 2019).

In many cases, pupils can hold both the 'misconception' and the scientific idea at the same time and may use different ways of explaining events in different situations (DFE, 2008). Some misconceptions may persist despite teachers' best efforts. Even when presented with new evidence, pupils may modify it to fit into their existing model.

Strategies for eliciting misconceptions

Before a misconception can be corrected, it needs to be identified. There are many different strategies a teacher can use to find out what misconceptions pupils may have. These ideas can include the following.

Questioning The most straightforward way is to ask the pupils directly and elicit their ideas in this way. This could be combined with mini whiteboards where all pupils can write their answer then hold it up. Diagnostic Question banks can also be used. The Best Evidence Science Teaching (BEST) pilot project is trialling a bank of diagnostic questions that can reveal misunderstandings.

Concept cartoons Brenda Keogh and Stuart Naylor pioneered the use of concept cartoons in the early 1990s to promote discussion, and elicit and challenge pupils' ideas. Concept cartoons are used to present a scientific concept within an everyday situation which a group of cartoon pupils are discussing. Different viewpoints are shown, which the pupils might agree or disagree with, creating cognitive conflict and revealing any misconceptions (Naylor, 2015).

Drawings Asking the pupils to draw or annotate a picture can give the teacher an idea of what the pupils are thinking. For example, if asked to draw different animals, do the pupils only draw four-legged animals, or do they include snakes/ fish/birds etc. (Allen, 2019)? These diagrams can be used as a basis for further questions.

Concept maps There are different ways to create concept maps. A simple way is for the teacher to provide all the key words for the pupils to cut out. Associated words are stuck down and linked with pencil lines. Each line is accompanied by a comment explaining why they are linked (Allen, 2019).

Websites such as Explorify also provide excellent resources that teachers can use to tease out misconceptions from a class – website details can be found in the Further reading and resources section at the end of this chapter.

See Chapter 14 for more on assessment.

Dealing with misconceptions

So how do you correct a misconception when you've found out what it is? It is important to challenge the ideas of the pupil in a non-threatening way (DfE, 2008). Pupils need to be able to test out their ideas to experience the 'cognitive conflict' in a non-threatening way. As teachers, we should not simply tell pupils that their ideas are wrong and explain what they should think instead, which will be counterproductive.

The challenge for a primary teacher is to organise the child's naive ideas and misconceptions into coherent concepts that are accurate and explicit. These misconceptions cannot be ignored since they are the foundations upon which new knowledge is built (Pine et al., 2001).

Link any intervention with prior knowledge. Introduce a situation where the misconception is shown, such as a clip from a movie showing loud explosions in space before explaining that sound cannot travel in a vacuum.

Investigating the concept through practical work can also help address the misconception. Pupils can make their prediction – what they think will happen and why they have reached that conclusion. They can then see if their prediction is correct. If their prediction is shown to be wrong, this can result in cognitive conflict. The pupil will then hopefully reject their wrong idea and assimilate the scientific concept.

For a comprehensive approach to dealing with a wide range of science misconceptions, I highly recommend reading *Misconceptions in Primary Science* by Michael Allen (2019).

Websites such as the Primary Science Teacher Trust and the PLAN Assessment Knowledge Matrices also have some good guides to common primary school misconceptions. Details of these websites among others can be found in the Further reading and resources section at the end of this chapter.

Models and analogies in science

Ideas are abstract concepts that cannot be seen. In order to communicate an idea, it has to be represented in some way. This could be through the use of words, symbols, actions, pictures, diagrams, models, and more (Asoko and De Boo, 2001). Science often involves pupils learning abstract concepts that might be contrary to what they expect (Ofsted, 2023). If the idea is to be communicated effectively, the representation needs to be well chosen, clear and concise.

Analogies, models and metaphors are all representations used by teachers when trying to explain a concept or an idea. These can be particularly helpful tools in science classrooms (Asoko and De Boo, 2001). When these models are used alongside clear explanations, they can help pupils to learn connected knowledge. However, all models need to be used with caution because they can lead to misconceptions (Ofsted, 2023).

To help children understand particular concepts, a teacher might introduce fun activities and role-play tasks where they act out particular phenomena – for example, they might model blood flow by moving around the playground in a figure of eight, or they might act out being the particles in a solid, liquid and gas. These models can be fun, and we will cover quite a few ideas later in this book, but they need to be used with caution. Asoko and de Boo (2001) outlined several difficulties in using representations, as well as things to consider.

Difficulties include:

- children may need additional support in linking the model to the target situation, particularly if it's very abstract;
- children may remember the fun activity they did, but not what it represents;
- irrelevant or misleading features may be incorporated into the new way of thinking, leading to more misconceptions;
- the representation is no replacement for the actual 'target' situation.

In selecting models to use with the children, teachers therefore need to consider the following questions:

- What is represented and how well?
- What is missing or not represented?
- What might be confusing?
- What are limitations of the model?
- Will children be able to understand it easily?
- Does it need prior knowledge?

Analogies as pedagogical tools each have their own strengths and limitations (Ramos, 2011), but they have potential if they are properly used. Often a single analogy won't be enough and presenting children with several models can aid understanding more than using a single model (Chiu and Lin 2005).

No model is perfect and it will usually fall down on some aspect of what actually happens in real life. However, the shortfalls could be discussed with the pupils who will need support in using any analogy to aid their understanding. The relationship between the parts of the model and what is being explained needs to be made explicit for them to make sense of the science behind the model (Ramos, 2011).

Sustainability and science

Science holds the answers to many of our world's sustainability issues, and scientists are carrying out crucial work in understanding and tackling threats such as climate change. Young people are particularly interested in green issues and embedding sustainability into the curriculum is a major step towards ensuring that children understand what their future holds, and maybe can help change things for the better in the future.

With that in mind, where appropriate in this book, I will flag up opportunities where the science curriculum can incorporate the 17 Sustainable Development Goals produced by the United Nations.

Further reading and resources

Best Evidence Science Teaching 7–11: www.stem.org.uk/primary/resources/collections/science/best-evidence-science-teaching
Explorify: https://explorify.uk

IOPSpark: Energy in the New Curriculum: https://spark.iop.org/collections/energy-new-curriculum

PLAN Assessment Knowledge Matrices: www.planassessment.com/plan-knowledge-matrices

Primary Science Teacher Trust, Common Misconceptions: https://pstt.org.uk/resources/common-misconceptions/

RSC – Sustainability for Contexts for Primary Science: https://edu.rsc.org/primary-science/sustainability-contexts-for-primary-science/4014614.article

United Nations 17 Sustainability Goals: https://sdgs.un.org/goals

WWF – Schools Sustainability Guide: www.wwf.org.uk/get-involved/schools/sustainability-guide

CHAPTER 2

Working Scientifically

Introduction

Working scientifically is a vital part of the primary science curriculum. It is a pedagogical approach that encourages children to engage with the world around them, fostering curiosity and engagement in science.

Working scientifically specifies the understanding of the nature, processes and methods of science for each year group. It's what children do to answer scientific questions about the world around them (Turner et al., 2011).

Practical work in science

High-quality practical work forms a vital part of a science education (Ofsted, 2023). This can take the form of both hands-on practical activities or teacher demonstrations. Practical work introduces pupils to the methods, objects and phenomena that scientists study. In turn, this develops pupils' sense of wonder and curiosity about the material world. Practical work also teaches pupils about the unpredictable nature of science and that they do not always get a clear answer.

According to Holman (2017), the purposes of practical science are summarised as follows.

- To teach the principles of scientific enquiry.
- To improve understanding of theory through practical experience.
- To teach specific practical skills, such as measurement and observation, that may be useful in future study or employment.

- To motivate and engage students.
- To develop higher level skills and attributes such as communication, teamwork and perseverance.

In schools, practical work is not always as effective as it could be. This might be because the purpose of the practical is not clear or because pupils are expected to do and think about too much at once. Practical work is effective when it has clear aims and when pupils have enough prior knowledge to learn from the activity. When this is not the case, pupils experience too much complexity, which prevents them from learning what was intended.

Disciplinary knowledge

Ofsted (2021) defines **disciplinary knowledge** in science as the use of methods, techniques, data and evidence to establish and refine scientific knowledge. Disciplinary knowledge encompasses the processes through which scientific knowledge is established and refined, and it is essential for a comprehensive and effective science curriculum. In principle, this is the working scientifically or 'doing science' strand of the curriculum and it includes how to carry out practical activities.

The science curriculum in a school should embed opportunities to develop disciplinary knowledge within the most appropriate substantive knowledge, providing a balanced approach to equipping children with the knowledge they need to build their understanding and demonstrate their scientific findings. Schools should not expect children to acquire disciplinary knowledge as a by-product of taking part in practical activities. These skills should be explicitly taught (Ofsted, 2023). Pupils should be taught how to carry out procedures such as measuring values and drawing a line graph.

In their 2023 report, Ofsted found that there was too much focus on developing pupils' disciplinary knowledge at the expense of how to develop their substantive knowledge. Not enough consideration was given to identifying the disciplinary knowledge that is needed to work scientifically. Too often, the focus was simply on identifying practical activities for pupils to complete.

Working scientifically should not be taught as a separate strand (DfE, 2013a), but should be embedded within science lessons across the curriculum.

Science enquiry skills

Scientific enquiry involves a range of skills that children need to develop and practise throughout their primary education. These skills include:

- **Observing** Using their senses to notice and describe what is happening around them.
- **Questioning** Asking questions about what they observe and what they want to find out more about.
- **Predicting** Making a guess or hypothesis about what might happen, based on their prior knowledge and experience.
- **Planning** Deciding how to carry out an investigation, what materials and equipment to use and, if applicable, how to ensure a fair test.
- **Measuring** Using appropriate units and tools to collect and record quantitative data.
- **Recording** Using different methods and formats to record their observations and data, such as tables, charts, graphs, diagrams and photographs.
- **Analysing** Interpreting and explaining their data, looking for patterns, trends and anomalies.
- **Evaluating** Reflecting on their investigation, identifying strengths and weaknesses, and suggesting improvements.
- **Communicating** Sharing their findings and conclusions with others, using oral, written and visual methods.

Children may use different skills at different stages of an investigation, and may revisit or revise their questions, predictions, plans or conclusions as they progress. The skills also vary in complexity and sophistication, depending on the age and ability of the children, and the nature and context of the investigation.

Through science enquiry activities, children will get the chance to use various pieces of scientific equipment, such as thermometers, balances or stopwatches for measurement. This may also include digital technologies, such as computers, tablets, dataloggers or cameras that can enhance the observation, measurement, recording and communication of data.

Progression of enquiry skills

Moving from lower to upper primary, pupils should become increasingly autonomous in their decision-making when carrying out investigations. They should become systematic and accurate in collecting and analysing data, and able to express their ideas scientifically using scientific language and enquiry.

The progression of skills KS1 to KS2 include:

- **Planning** Move from beginning to think of their own ideas for experiments to suggesting questions to test and plan their own experiments. Move from saying what they think will happen to explaining their predictions in more detail.
- **Carrying out** Begin by making simple observations. Start to take simple measurements of things such as time, length, mass. Later, use a range of equipment with increasing accuracy and present results in the most appropriate way.
- **Analysing** Begin by drawing simple charts and later make comparisons with a range of different charts and graphs. Attempt to link their prediction to what they found out. Later use their results to suggest further experiments to be tested.
- **Evaluating** In KS2, begin to identify results that do not seem to fit the pattern observed. Decide when observations need to be repeated to improve reliability.

These skills are not innate or fixed, but are learned and developed through practice and feedback. These skills also vary in complexity and sophistication, depending on the age and ability of the students, and the nature and context of the enquiry. Therefore, teachers should ensure continuity and progression of essential enquiry skills across the curriculum and the key stages, and they need to provide students with a variety of experiences and opportunities to practise and apply their skills across different areas of science and beyond (Harlen and Qualter, 2018).

Types of investigation

The nature of the scientific investigation will vary according to the type of questions being explored. The most common type seen in schools is the 'fair test' (AKSIS, 2004), but this is not the only option and other types of science enquiry activity may be better suited to answer different kinds of questions. Pattern seeking and using secondary sources are underused in primary schools (Ofsted, 2023).

Sometimes the lines between the different types of enquiry might be blurred, and a fair test might involve some observation over time or research, for example.

An excellent guide to the range of scientific enquiry is *It's Not Fair, or Is It?* by Turner et al. (2011).

Fair tests

In this type of enquiry, the children identify the relationship between variables. They will explore the effect that changing one variable has on another variable, while all others are kept the same.

There are many occasions when a fair test is the best method for the question being asked, such as finding out which surface is the best for stopping a runaway car at the bottom of a ramp. The size of car, height of the ramp and position the car is let go from should all be kept the same. Only the material at the bottom of the ramp should be changed (sand, grass, carpet, gravel, etc.). They measure the other variable, the distance travelled by the car at the bottom of the ramp and use these results to come up with their answer.

- **Independent variable** The thing that is changed during the experiment.
- **Dependent variable** The thing that is observed or measured during the experiment.
- **Controlled variables** The things that are kept the same throughout the experiment.

Observing over time

This type of enquiry involves taking measurements or observations over a few days, a week or even longer. It could be used when growing seeds or bulbs, or monitoring seasonal changes.

Think about how the children will collect their data. Should you provide them with a data-collection sheet with boxes ready for them to enter their observations?

Examples include: 'How will the seeds that we've planted change over time?' or 'How long will it take for this biodegradable bag to break down if we bury it?'

Identifying and classifying

Identifying and classifying helps us make sense of the world by looking at how it is organised. Children can put things into different groups based on observable properties or features.

Children could sort objects into groups using hoops or circles drawn on large sheets of paper. For more advanced grouping, the hoops could overlap to form a Venn diagram. Encourage the children to talk and describe the different objects and to explain the reasons for their choices.

Examples include: 'Which clothes will keep us cool in the summer and which will keep us warm in the winter?' or 'Which materials are magnetic or non-magnetic?'

Pattern seeking

In pattern seeking, children are looking for patterns in sets of data. This can be data they have collected themselves or secondary data from other sources. For example, 'Does foot size relate to height in humans?' or 'Which parts of the school has the most litter?'

Sometimes a pattern is quite obvious, like the relationship between the size of the bar of a xylophone and the pitch of the note it makes. Sometimes, there may be a relationship between two things, but one does not cause the other such as height vs. foot size. At other times, there may be no pattern at all.

Research (using secondary sources)

This type of enquiry involves using secondary sources such as books and the internet to answer questions that would prove difficult to test in the classroom. For example: 'Which planet in the solar system is the coldest?'

Researching using secondary sources can provide opportunities to practise different skills (Turner et al., 2011), such as:

- Comparing and evaluating information from different sources.
- Distinguishing fact from opinion and recognising bias.
- Recognising questions that don't have definite answers.

There are opportunities for links to be made here to the computing curriculum in using search technologies effectively and evaluating digital content. A good starting point to test the children on this is the 'Save the Pacific Northwest Tree Octopus' website, which is completely fake, but very convincing!

Ensure that the children are guided in the use of which websites to use, and that the ones they use are age-appropriate. Don't just let them loose on Google, but give them specific sites to use, or use a child-friendly search engine like DuckDuckGo or Kiddle.

To help collect and organise the information, it might be an idea to use scaffolded data-collection sheets or graphic organisers (see Figure 2.1) to prevent wholesale copy and pasting from sites such as Wikipedia.

Name of planet:		Planet Research
How far is it from the Sun?	**How many moons has it got?**	It is the ____ planet from the Sun.
		Draw a picture of it
How long is a day?	**How long is a year?**	
Gas giant or rocky planet?	**Other interesting facts:**	

Figure 2.1   An example of a graphic organiser to support a research task

Problem solving

Problem solving is when the children apply prior scientific knowledge to find answers to problems. Children can be challenged with a situation and asked to work out how best to solve it.

Children might be given the challenge of designing a balloon-powered car that can travel the furthest or designing a protective casing for an egg to allow it to survive a 2-metre drop to the floor.

In answering the question, the children might draw on several different enquiry types. For example, to design the best balloon car might involve fair testing, changing the size or material of the wheels to see what effect this has on distance.

Sometimes this might involve a crime scene investigation activity where different forensic skills are used to decide who committed a crime, such as chromatography, fingerprinting and studying footprints.

Note

If you do try using a crime scene investigator (CSI) event, keep the crime low level, such as the kidnap of the class teddy or the theft of a class reading book. Trying a crime scene like 'the caretaker has been murdered' is a surefire way to end up being reported in the *Daily Mail*!

Planning for science enquiry

Ofsted says that the most effective science teachers make it a priority to maintain curiosity in their pupils (Ofsted, 2013), and making this a key principle of working scientifically by enquiry can be very beneficial in helping pupils see themselves as scientists. Curiosity and imagination should stimulate questions, predictions and hypotheses. It is then the teacher's role to enable the children to investigate and test out these ideas (McCrory, 2017).

Teachers need to carefully select practical tasks that are appropriate and challenging for their students, and scaffold and support their learning (Limón, 2001). If the task is too easy, the children will be bored. If it is too difficult, the children won't be able to engage with productive enquiry.

Teachers should ensure that all pupils have opportunities to take part in high-quality practical work with a clear purpose (Ofsted, 2023). The children may look busy, but are they actually learning? Consider the purpose of the practical activity – is the objective clear and could it be carried out in any other ways? Have the children been taught the necessary scientific knowledge to be able to explain what they find out in the practical activity?

Don't always feel that every science practical has to involve the pupils in planning out a full investigation from start to finish. Do have lessons where the objective focuses on a single skill area, such as planning an experiment or drawing conclusions.

For more on planning a science practical, see Chapter 13.

Effective group work

Practical work is best carried out in groups. Each child can be allocated a particular role in a group, and each member should have the chance to fully participate in the activity. Because of the limited number of roles available, groups larger than four can make practical work difficult.

Specific roles could include:

- **Recorder** Takes notes and records group processes.
- **Measurer** Takes readings and measurements.
- **Timekeeper** Monitors the time spent on a task.

- **Gopher/runner** Collects the apparatus and resources needed to complete a task. Also fetches teacher if needed.
- **Researcher** Collects background information needed to complete a task.
- **Checker** Checks that facts are correct.
- **Summariser** Summarises conclusions and prepares the group's presentation to the class.

Collecting and presenting data

Ways of collecting data

Younger pupils will simply observe events rather than measure or compare them. At this level, pupils can look for changes and describe what has happened. Older pupils may still use observations when relevant, but they should be moving more towards taking measurements using the correct units.

When working in groups, pupils could be allocated roles so that there is a 'measurer' who is taking the readings and a 'scribe' who is writing them down on a results sheet. Swap these roles around regularly.

Data-collecting equipment

At a basic level, tables can be used to collect readings and observations. Older pupils could construct these themselves, but blank table scaffolds can be provided to give pupils a guide. Digital technologies can be helpful too.

For more on digital technologies, see Chapter 16.

Presenting data

There are different ways to present their findings, depending on the type of data collected and the skills that have been taught in maths/numeracy lessons.

Young pupils could draw simple pictograms with assistance. Lower primary should be able to start drawing simple bar charts, although they may need support choosing a suitable scale. Upper primary should be able to draw line and scatter graphs. Some pupils may need scaffolding to help produce charts and tables, and these may be presented to them partially completed, whereas other pupils would be expected to create these from scratch.

Simple spreadsheets or databases could also be set up to draw graphs based on the data inputted by the pupils. This could be a good way to collect whole-class data to be presented on the screen at the front of the class or shared via the Cloud for all pupils to then access. For example, collecting data on the height, eye colour and hair colour of the class which they can then all access to produce graphs and charts.

Further reading and resources

CIEC – Skills for Science – Centre for Industry Education Collaboration: www.york.ac.uk/ciec/resources/primary/skills-for-science

Enquiring science 4 all: https://seerih-innovations.org/enquiringscience4all

Primary Science Teacher Trust: Enquiry Approaches: https://pstt.org.uk/resources/curriculum-materials/enquiry-approaches

Primary Science Teacher Trust: Science Skills: https://pstt.org.uk/resources/curriculum-materials/enquiry-skills

Save the Pacific Northwest Tree Octopus: https://zapatopi.net/treeoctopus

The Great Science Share for Schools: www.greatscienceshare.org

CHAPTER 3

Science in English Primary Schools: Where Are We?

Introduction

Although the national curriculum outlines the statutory requirements for teaching science, the delivery and quality of science teaching in primary schools vary widely across the country. All schools are facing many challenges and gaps that need to be addressed and overcome, such as pressures of time, funding and teacher retention. On top of this, they are still dealing with the effects of the pandemic when we had to lock down schools and try to teach remotely.

The delivery and quality of science education in primary school

The delivery and quality of science education in primary schools vary widely across England, as evidenced by various reports such as those produced by the Wellcome Trust and Ofsted.

Curriculum time and coverage Science is a core subject, but since it is no longer examined as part of the KS2 SATs, time is often reduced to make way for more literacy and numeracy (Ofsted, 2021). The average time spent on science in UK primary schools is 1 hour and 42 minutes per week, below the recommended two hours per week (Wellcome, 2019).

Teacher expertise and confidence Very few primary teachers could be considered a science specialist by background. Only 5 per cent of primary teachers have a science-related degree, and 25 per cent of teachers are concerned that they may not be able to answer children's questions about science (Wellcome, 2019; Ofsted, 2023).

Resources and equipment Funding and resourcing is an issue in primary school. Some schools did not have enough or appropriate resources and equipment for science (Ofsted, 2023). An unscientific poll I conducted among science leads recently put the average science budget at below £5 per pupil per year.

Assessment and feedback A total of 83 per cent of teachers assess pupils' science learning at least once a term (Wellcome, 2017). Some schools do not have a clear and consistent approach to assessing science, and some teachers do not use assessment information to identify and address pupils' misconceptions or gaps in learning (Ofsted, 2023).

Outcomes and impact Some 80 per cent of pupils reached the expected standard in science at the end of Key Stage 2 in 2023 (DFE, 2023). However, there seems to be a significantly widening attainment gap between disadvantaged pupils and their peers, particularly as a result of the pandemic (EPI, 2023).

Key issues for children's learning in science

In a report for the University of Manchester and The Ogden Trust, Bianchi et al. (2021) identified ten key issues that affect children's learning in primary school science.
These are:

1. Children's science learning is superficial and lacks depth.
2. Children's preconceptions aren't adequately valued.
3. Children's science learning lacks challenge.
4. Children are over-reliant on teacher talk and direction; they lack autonomy and independence in learning science.
5. Children experience 'fun' science activities that fail to deepen or develop new learning.
6. Children are not encouraged to use their own curiosity, scientific interests and questions in their science learning.
7. Children are engaged in prescriptive practical work that lacks purpose.
8. Children do not draw on their learning from prior scientific skills; they do not build on repeated and regular experiences.
9. Children rarely see themselves, their families, community members or their teachers as scientists.
10. Children do not apply literacy and numeracy skills in science at the standard they use in English and mathematics.

Improving primary science: the EEF review, 2023

A comprehensive review of the approaches to primary science teaching was carried out by Bennett et al. (2023) on behalf of the Education Endowment Foundation. This informed the recommendations contained in the Improving Primary Science Guidance Report (2023).

The report makes six recommendations, each outlining a common challenge faced by primary science teachers.

The summary of recommendations is as follows:

1. **Develop pupils' scientific vocabulary**

   - Identify science-specific vocabulary.
   - Explicitly teach new vocabulary and its meaning, creating opportunities for repeated engagement and use over time.

2. **Encourage pupils to explain their thinking whether verbally or in written form**

   - Create a collaborative learning environment.
   - Capitalise on the power of dialogue.
   - Cultivate reasoning and justification.

3. **Guide pupils to work scientifically**

   - Explicitly teach the knowledge and skills required to work scientifically, guiding pupils to apply this in practice with opportunities for discussion and reflection.

4. **Relate new learning to relevant real-world contexts**

   - Consider real-world contexts.
   - Engage with science concepts supported by virtual models.

5. **Use assessment to support teaching and responsive teaching**

   - Plan teaching that builds on existing knowledge and experiences.
   - Monitor pupils' learning to inform responsive teaching, feedback and next steps.
   - Summarise what pupils have learned against planned criteria.

6. **Strengthen science teaching through effective professional development**

   - Use a range of information to identify development priorities and professional learning needs.

- Consider factors of high-quality professional development to plan or evaluate provision.
- Reflect on senior leadership support at the strategic to classroom level.

Enhancing teacher expertise and confidence in science

It is important to provide teachers with adequate and relevant professional development and support, and with opportunities to share and learn from their peers and experts (Wellcome, 2014, 2021). Ensuring that all teachers have access and entitlement to high-quality and ongoing CPD in science – for example, using websites such as STEM Learning or Reach Out CPD. Teachers could join professional learning communities and networks in science, such as the ASE's regional and local groups, and STEM Learning's online community.

Improving resources and equipment for science

Teachers and pupils need to have access to adequate resources and equipment for teaching and learning science, such as apparatus, technology and facilities (Wellcome, 2021). Charities such as The Ogden Trust can support schools with specialist physics kit. Schools may sometimes be able to borrow resources from local secondary schools. Science subject leaders should have strategic responsibility for a dedicated science budget (Wellcome, 2014).

Further reading and resources

Explorify: https://explorify.uk
Gatsby Foundation: www.gatsby.org.uk
Nuffield Foundation: www.nuffieldfoundation.org
The Ogden Trust: www.ogdentrust.com
Primary Science Quality Mark: www.herts.ac.uk/psqm/psqm
Primary Science Teacher Trust: https://pstt.org.uk
Reach Out CPD: www.reachoutcpd.com
Science Fix: www.sciencefix.com
STEM Learning: www.stem.org.uk

PART 2

CHAPTER 4

Plants

Introduction

Plants as a separate topic exists in Years 1, 2 and 3 before becoming part of other units such as habitats and life cycles. It's a good way to introduce children to their local environment, as they can study local plants that grow in the school grounds, as well as inexpensive plants that can be brought into the classroom.

It has been suggested that children growing up in the UK today are more disconnected from nature than any previous generation (Harris, 2023). Studying the plants around us can stimulate an interest in nature and the local environment. It can also provide opportunities for taking the science out of the classroom and into the real world.

It also gives the children an opportunity to grow things from seeds and bulbs, as many children don't get to see this happen at home. It should be pointed out that there is more to plants than growing cress, though, and this should not be something they do every year.

This unit also links nicely with seasonal changes as children can observe how the local plants change over the course of a year.

Science knowledge you need before you can teach this topic

Identifying and naming plants

Within the KS1 science national curriculum, there is an expectation that children are able to identify some of the plants in your local environment. There is no statutory list of plants that the children should know, so you can use whatever trees you have in and around the school grounds.

Make yourself aware of the common trees you might find in your school grounds. They can be easily identified by their leaf shapes and their fruits in the autumn. These include oak, beech, sycamore, silver birch, Scots pine and horse chestnut.

Be hands-on in developing the children's understanding of plants and allow them to handle and examine the leaves and fruits of these trees (acorns, conkers, etc.). They can sort them into groups based on different features. Teaching this unit in the autumn term makes it easier to gather them from the outdoors than it is trying to teach it in January.

Tip

An easy way to reinforce the most common tree names would be to name your class tables after them. Hang the name of the tree, and an image of its leaf and fruit above each table.

Comprehensive guides and keys to identify common British plants can be easily found online such as the Tree Tools for Schools guides from the Woodland Trust (for full details, see the Further reading and resources section at the end of this chapter). You can also get apps for your phone that will try to identify most plants and trees from a photograph of the leaf or a flower such as LeafSnap, PlantSnap or even Google Lens.

Remember: trees don't move! The trees you find in your school grounds will stay the same for many years. Make a labelled plan of the trees around your school, keep it handy and you'll be able to use it year after year. Include it in your planning folder and pass it on to colleagues if they take over your class.

Deciduous or evergreen?

Trees and shrubs can be broadly grouped into those that are deciduous or those that are evergreen. Deciduous plants lose their leaves seasonally, usually before the winter or dry season. Because water is lost from the leaves, losing them allows the plant to conserve water.

Evergreen plants keep their leaves throughout the year. An evergreen plant gradually loses and replaces leaves all the time, but there is no point in the year where it has no leaves. Evergreens include holly as well as most species of conifer tree, such as spruce, cedar and pine.

Structure of a plant

In Key Stage 1, the four key organs of a plant that children are required to know are the roots, stem, leaves and flowers.

Roots The roots absorb water and nutrients and store these for the plant. The roots also anchor the plant in the ground and prevent it from falling over.

Stem The role of the stem is to transport water and minerals from the roots up to the leaves and flower. It also transports food away from the leaves to the rest of the plant. The stem also supports the plant, keeping it upright.

Leaves The leaves contain chlorophyll and are responsible for the process of photosynthesis in green plants, where the plant makes its food.

Flower The part of a plant responsible for reproduction. They contain eggs and make pollen. Some flowers are bright and colourful to attract insects to spread their pollen. Other flowers are less attractive and release pollen onto the wind to float through the air.

The flowers produce fruits, which contain seeds. As well as the things we automatically think of as fruits, such as apples and pears, it also includes fruits such as acorns and conkers.

Germinating seeds

In Year 2 plants, the children are introduced to growing seeds and bulbs. They can plant seeds such as broad beans and cress, and observe what happens when they germinate. They can also plant bulbs such as crocus or daffodil.

Germination is when a seed starts to grow into a new plant. Seeds don't always start growing right away. They need the right conditions to germinate. Seeds need water, oxygen and the correct temperature. Seeds don't need light or soil to germinate.

Germinating cress

Cress is often grown in the classroom because it germinates really quickly. You can easily sow it on damp cotton wool or a paper towel. Cress grown in the dark will be tall and thin because it is trying to find the light. Once it is exposed to the light, it will turn darker green and grow normally.

Don't just grow cress every year – try some other seeds as well. Other seeds that are good for growing in the classroom include mustard and beans. Large seeds such as peas, sunflowers and sweetcorn work well. Remember that store-bought seeds might be dusted with chemicals, such as fungicide, so children should always wash their hands after handling them, and they should never eat the seeds. When bringing plants and seeds into the classroom, be aware of any allergies the children in your class might have.

To read more about health and safety considerations, see Chapter 18.

The Science and Plants for Schools (SAPS) website produces some excellent guides to all aspects of teaching about plants and I highly recommend taking a look at it. Details can be found in the Further reading and resources section at the end of this chapter.

What do plants need to stay alive?

After they have germinated, the most important things that plants need to stay healthy are **sunlight, warmth, water and air (carbon dioxide and oxygen)**. Sunlight provides the energy for photosynthesis, the process of converting carbon dioxide and water into glucose, which the plant uses as food. Plants obtain carbon dioxide from the air around them and water from the soil.

The word equation for photosynthesis is:

Carbon dioxide + water → glucose + oxygen

Most of the mass of a plant comes from the carbon dioxide in the air, which is incorporated into the glucose molecules.

Like all other living things, plants also need oxygen, since they need to respire the glucose they produce within all their cells. This releases energy and allows the plants to carry out all the things it needs to do to stay alive.

Plants do not actually need soil to stay healthy. They can be grown in water with added minerals and nutrients, which is called 'hydroponics'.

Pupils can carry out simple experiments to see how plants grow in different conditions. Place mature plants (not seeds!) in warm/cold and light/dark places and give plants different amounts of water and fertilisers to see what happens. Plants like basil are inexpensive when bought at a supermarket and work well for this, but you can also use more typical house plants such as geraniums. These experiments can run over several weeks, so keep this in mind when planning lessons. Time should be allocated to check in and record the progress of the plants and to talk about conclusions at the end of the session.

Note

At primary level, the children would not be expected to know the word 'photosynthesis' but should simply be aware that plants 'make their own food', and that this needs sunlight to happen. Personally, however, I think it would be a good idea to introduce the word in KS2 and look at science root words such as 'photo', meaning light. In doing so, we can help children to use the correct scientific vocabulary.

Water transport in plants

Water is absorbed by the roots in the soil. This water travels up the stem to the leaves. Water is sucked up through the stem through tiny tubes, called **xylem**, very much like water is sucked up through a straw. This sucking force is caused by water leaving the leaves by evaporation. This is called transpiration. As water evaporates from the leaves, more water is sucked up from the roots. Water is constantly moving through plants.

Other tubes called **phloem** carry water containing glucose away from the leaves to the rest of the plant. Water in the stem keeps the plant upright. If a plant does not get enough water, it will wilt and eventually die.

You can observe the movement of water by placing a plant such as celery or white carnations into water containing bright food colouring. Be sure to cut the stems very cleanly at the bottom with a knife. After a few hours, the children will see the flowers or celery leaves change colour. You can even cut the celery across the stem and see the coloured dots which show where the tubes are (if you snap the celery, you might even reveal some of the tough, stringy tubes with colour in them).

Tip

I have found that the liquid and gel food colouring that you often find in supermarkets doesn't work in this experiment. If you can, buy powdered food colouring online which produces much better results.

Plant reproduction

Flowers contain the parts a plant needs to reproduce. Most plants have both male and female reproductive organs. Flowers have brightly coloured petals and a nice smell which attract insects. They often produce a sweet liquid called nectar to make it worthwhile for the insects to visit.

The male part of a flower is called the **stamen**. It is made of thin hairs called filaments, with a bulbous end called the anther. The anthers produce the pollen.

Pollen grains are as tiny as specks of dust, and they contain the male genetic material – half the information needed to make a whole new plant.

The female parts of the plant are called the **carpel** (or pistil). They are made up of the stigma, style and ovary. Inside the ovary are tiny eggs which also contain half the information needed to make a new plant.

Tip

Buy bunches of cut flowers so that children can look at their structure. Tulips are good to use as an example, and reasonably inexpensive, when available. As an alternative, try alstroemeria. Lilies are also good as they have large anthers and stamen, but the pollen can be a problem as it stains easily, and some children can be allergic to it. Digital microscopes and hand lenses will be useful for taking a closer look at the structure of flowers.

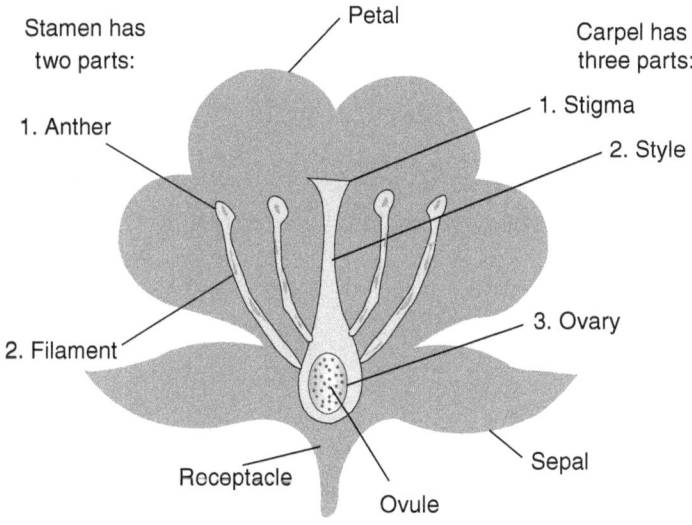

Stamen has
two parts:

1. Anther

2. Filament

Petal

Carpel has
three parts:

1. Stigma

2. Style

3. Ovary

Receptacle

Ovule

Sepal

Figure 4.1   The parts of a flower

Pollination

The transfer of pollen from an anther to a stigma is called pollination. The pollen travels from the anther of one flower, and then eventually lands on the stigma of another flower. This can be carried out by insects or by the wind.

Once the pollen has landed on the stigma, it grows a tube down the style to the ovary where it joins with the egg to fertilise it. The egg now has a complete set of genetic information needed to make a new plant.

Pollination vs. fertilisation

There is often confusion between the process of pollination and fertilisation. Although they are closely linked, they are two separate processes. Pollination is the process by which the pollen gets from one flower to another. Once the pollen is on the other flower, it can then fertilise the ovule. The pollen joins with the ovule to create an embryo that develops into a seed. One grain of pollen and one ovule are needed for each seed that is produced.

Sustainability link

Make links to biodiversity. Look at the importance of pollinators such as bees and butterflies.

Could they create a good habitat for bees in a small corner of the school grounds? Can they find out what kinds of plants are best for attracting bees? Perhaps plant a wildflower strip.

Fruits

Once the eggs are fertilised, the ovary swells up. The eggs develop into seeds and the ovary develops into a fruit. The petals fall off. Next time you eat an apple, take a look at the bottom of it. You can still see the remains of the flower at the very end.

When you're eating a strawberry, an apple or even a courgette or pumpkin, you are eating what used to be the ovary of the flower. All of these are technically fruits.

A common mistake is that in everyday language the word 'fruit' is used to refer only to sweet-tasting plant products like apples, oranges and bananas. However, the botanical definition of fruit – the ripened ovaries of a flowering plant – encompasses many types of vegetables as well, such as tomato, cucumber, peas, beans and peppers.

Seed dispersal

Plants **disperse** their seeds in many different ways. They can glide on the wind, float on water or even explode to hurl their seeds into the air.

Many plants also use animals to carry their seeds. Some have hooks which can attach themselves to an animal's fur. Other seeds have evolved to look and taste pleasant so that animals will eat them. The seeds can survive the journey through the digestive system and will pass out the other end with a nice lump of fertiliser to help them on their way – exactly like sweetcorn, before you ask!

The plant life cycle

The plant life cycle has five main stages.

- **Germination** The seed germinates and begins to grow.
- **Growth** The seedling grows into a mature plant.

- **Flowering** The flowers form and produce eggs and pollen. Pollination can now take place, which leads to fertilisation.
- **Seed formation** The fertilised eggs now develop into seeds. The ovary swells up and forms a fruit to protect the seed.
- **Seed dispersal** The seeds are spread out to new places to grow.

Not all plants make seeds, though; non-flowering plants like conifers and ferns produce spores instead.

Challenges and misconceptions the children may have

There is often confusion about what actually is a plant. Young children often describe plants as having flowers with coloured petals, green leaves and a stem. There are many plants that children might not immediately think of as plants since they don't have flowers such as mosses and ferns. Adding to the confusion, they may have heard gardening parents differentiating between plants and weeds, so children might think that there is a difference between the two.

Pupils will often think that mushrooms and toadstools are plants, but these do not have chlorophyll and can't make their own food, and so they are in their own kingdom called fungi. It is worth noting that algae, including seaweeds, are also not part of the plant kingdom since they do not have roots, stems or leaves, although they do photosynthesise. Instead, they belong to a different kingdom of living things called the protoctista (or protists).

Many pupils think that plants get their food from the soil. This is not helped by gardeners talking about fertiliser as 'plant food'. While it is true that a plant needs other chemicals such as magnesium and nitrates to make proteins and chlorophyll, these are not classed as food in the scientific sense. A food is something that supplies a living thing with energy. For plants, this is glucose which they make themselves via the process known as photosynthesis.

Making the learning real: linking the unit to everyday life

When teaching this topic, it would be useful to relate this topic to real examples that the children would have experienced. Some children may already have grown vegetables or sunflowers with their parents and can share what they know with the class.

With our urban lifestyles, many children don't know where the food they eat actually comes from. By growing common seeds such as beans and tomatoes, children can gain an understanding of the processes involved in getting fruit and vegetables onto their plates. Children often find it difficult to make the link between a flower and a fruit. It will help to directly observe this process happen by growing peppers or tomatoes. You could also observe changes in flowers already in the school grounds, such as roses or even blackberries.

It would be useful to have some potted plants in the classroom which the children can take turns to look after. Does the school have a nature area or a school garden that can be used as a resource? Are there any fun or interesting plants you can bring in or keep in the classroom such as cacti or air plants?

Sustainability link

Observing seasonal changes of local plants. How are we able to have fruit in our shops all year round? How far does some of it travel? Find where different things like tomatoes and avocados come from on a map.

Practical lesson ideas

Cress heads

Take clean yoghurt pots and paint faces on them. Put cotton wool inside the pots and sprinkle with cress seeds. Add enough water to make the cotton wool damp. Leave for a few days, watering occasionally. The cress should grow and make hair!

Mystery seeds

Explore the wide variety of seeds. Give examples from the very small, such as cress or poppy seeds, larger seeds such as peach stones or conkers, and the very large ones such as coconuts. You could present the children with a 'mystery seed' – perhaps from a tomato or pumpkin. Ask the children to discuss and guess what kind of plant it might grow into. Plant it in some soil and see what happens.

Care: wash hands after handling seeds from packets. Be aware of children with allergies.

Design a plant

Ask the children to design and build their own plant using common materials such as cardboard tubes, cake cases, tin foil, tissue paper, drinking straws, pipe cleaners and paper plates.

Leaf prints

Collect different leaves from plants around the school. The children can use these leaves to make pictures. Paint one side of a leaf with poster paint, press the painted side down onto a piece of white paper and then peel back. Repeat with different shapes and sizes of leaves, and different colours.

Cross-curricular links and opportunities

There are plenty of opportunities for cross-curricular work with literacy. The growing of seeds can be linked to stories like Jack and the Beanstalk. Children could write their own stories or poems about from the viewpoint of the magic beans. They could write instructions for looking after plants or growing seeds, perhaps including them on a design for a packet of seeds.

Plants can provide many opportunities to include maths skills. Children can look for patterns of symmetry in leaves, flowers and fruits. They could count the petals on a flower or lobes on a leaf and see what is the most common. Children could use leaves as a focus for estimating skills; they could estimate the area, perimeter and length/width of different leaves and then measure them.

In geography, they could find out which countries produce different fruits and vegetables, and find them on a map. Which travel the furthest? What are the 'air miles' of a typical school lunch?

Progression

The study of plants begins with the simple structure of plants and what they need to stay healthy. This progresses into exploring how plants reproduce, first sexually and later asexually, and the role of flowers. There are links to other units which look at habitats, plant classification and adaptation to the environment.

Suggested scientists

There are a great many plant scientists who could be featured here and that children might like to research. Some examples include:

- **Joseph Banks** Studied many plants on his travels around the world.
- **George Washington Carver** Developed crop rotation techniques to enrich the soil, helping peanuts to become a very important crop in America.
- **Agnes Arber** Plant anatomist. Only the third woman to be made a Fellow of the Royal Society. First to receive the Linnean Gold Medal from the Linnean Society.
- **Ahmed Mumin Warfa** Discovered many new Somalian plant species, including cyclamen.

Further reading and resources

Kew Gardens: Endeavour Plant Resources: https://endeavour.kew.org/home

Royal Horticultural Society: Campaign for School Gardening: https://schoolgardening.rhs.org.uk/home

Science and Plants for Schools: Primary Teaching Resources: www.saps.org.uk/teaching-resources/resources/?grouping=primary

STEM Learning: Plants: www.stem.org.uk/resources/community/collection/12535/year-3-plants

Wellcome: Darwin's Lookouts: www.stem.org.uk/elibrary/collection/4100

Woodland Trust – Tree Tools for Schools: www.treetoolsforschools.org.uk/

CHAPTER 5

Living Things and Habitats

Introduction

Life on Earth exists as a balance of living communities of organisms, interacting with each other and with their physical environment. Plants use sunlight to create food and oxygen. Animals need this oxygen and get their food either directly from eating plants or from eating other animals which have eaten plants. When these animals and plants die, decomposers break their bodies down so that the chemicals locked inside them can be recycled and reused. All these living things depend on each other for their survival.

Planet Earth is the only planet that we know of that can support life. It is currently the only home we have and we need to look after it. By teaching children about the environment and the impact of our actions, hopefully we can inspire future conservationists who can help protect it before it's too late.

Science knowledge you need before you can teach this topic

Living, dead or has never been alive?

It's a big question: 'What makes something alive?' As far as we know right now, our planet is the only one in the universe that has life on it. But if we do eventually travel to distant planets or moons, how will we know if we've discovered life? What would alien life look like?

Take a look outside if you can. Can you see any other living things, like trees or birds? How do you know they're alive? What are the characteristics of a living thing? In Year 2, the children need to be able to group things into living, dead and never been alive.

Children are often confused about what makes something a living thing. Something that moves fast that they can interact with, such as a family pet, is definitely alive. Something slow moving such as a bush or a daffodil may not be considered to be alive. Piaget (1929) observed that even children as old as 9 or 10 might think that things that move, such as a toy car or robot, could be mistaken for a living thing. A thing might be considered alive if it has blood, or makes a noise, or is warm. This can lead to misconceptions that the common animals they see around them are clearly alive, but things such as plants are not.

There can also be confusion in younger children between things that were once living and are now no longer alive, such as wood, and something that has never been alive such as stone. It can help to try to track back to where that material came from. Wood, and therefore also paper, was once part of a tree, but a stone has never been part of a living thing. Chalk is made from tiny animal shells, so it can be classed as dead.

Characteristics of living things

All living organisms have the potential to do these seven things:

- **M**ovement
- **R**espiration
- **S**ensing
- **G**rowth
- **R**eproduction
- **E**xcretion
- **N**utrition (feeding).

While some of this vocabulary is not suitable for Year 2, it can help you as a teacher to understand these characteristics. A simple mnemonic to help you remember them is '**MRS GREN**'.

It might not always be obvious that they are doing them – for example, plants may not move very much (but they do move!) and not everything might reproduce, but the potential is there.

Something like a toy robot may be able to move and sense, but it can't have babies or grow. Something like fire is very interesting as it can respire, feed, grow, excrete and reproduce, but it isn't able to sense and respond to its environment.

Grouping living things

Scientists have identified roughly 1.5 million different species of living things (not including bacteria), but this is a tiny fraction of the total biodiversity of life on Earth.

In Year 4, pupils explore how to group living things such as animals and plants. This would involve sorting animals into vertebrates and invertebrates. Plants can be grouped into flowering and non-flowering plants.

Tip

Introduce classification first by presenting images of various animals and plants. Ask the children to sort them using rules they come up with themselves as a group, such as they have wings and can fly or lives in water. This can generate good discussions among them. Later, you can introduce the idea of what rules other scientists have come up with that make a mammal a mammal or an insect an insect. They can resort using these rules.

Invertebrates

To classify animals, scientists can begin by taking a look at whether an animal has a backbone or not. The earliest creatures had no backbone (or any form of internal skeleton) and this was something that evolved later.

Animals that have no backbone are known as **invertebrates**. Some invertebrates, such as insects and crustaceans, have a hard exoskeleton, while others, like jellyfish, are supported by water. Invertebrates are subdivided into smaller groups according to similar features.

There are many groups of invertebrates, but the main ones to cover at a primary level include:

- **Insects** Have three body parts: head, thorax and abdomen. They also have six legs and two antennae. Includes bees, butterflies and ladybirds.
- **Arachnids** Usually have four pairs of legs and no antennae or wings. Includes spiders and scorpions.
- **Crustaceans** Generally, have two body parts and two pairs of antennae. The number of legs can vary. Typically, it can be ten, but can be more. Includes woodlice, crabs and lobsters.
- **Molluscs** Have a soft body and may have a shell. Includes slugs, snails, barnacles and octopus.
- **Myriapods** Have a long body with many segments and numerous legs. Includes centipedes and millipedes. Centipedes do not necessarily have a hundred legs!

- **Worms** Have a long soft body with many segments and no legs. Includes earth-worms.

These would be the kinds of invertebrate you might find in the school grounds on a minibeast hunt (see later). You might also like to introduce other interesting inverte-brates such as jellyfish, starfish, sponges and coral.

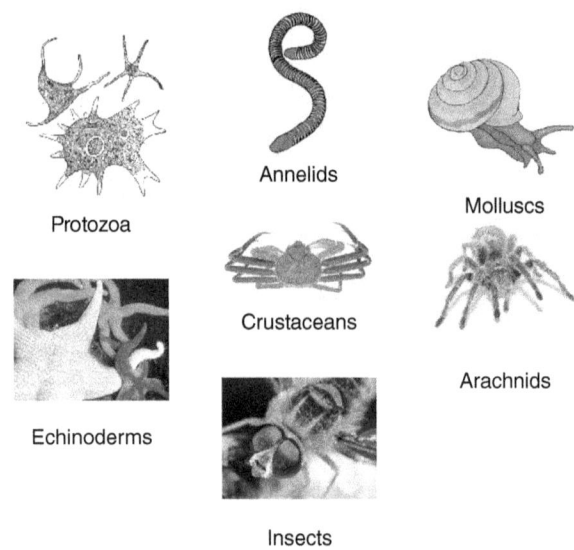

Figure 5.1   Invertebrates: animals without backbones

Vertebrates

Vertebrates are animals with bony spinal columns or backbones containing a spinal cord. They usually have a hard skull enclosing the brain and eyes.

Vertebrates are divided into five main groups based on their features. Children should be able to classify vertebrates into the following groups:

- **Mammals** These have fur and are warm-blooded. They give birth to live young that initially are fed by milk from the mother. The embryos develop inside a womb and are attached to the mother via an umbilical cord. They don't lay eggs. Examples of mammals include humans, dogs, whales and rabbits.
- **Birds** These have feathers and lay eggs with hard shells. They are warm-blooded and have wings and two legs. All modern birds have a beak with no teeth. All birds have wings, but not all birds can fly. Examples of birds include blackbirds, sparrows, penguins and seagulls.

- **Fish** Fish live in water, breathe through gills and have no limbs with digits. Fish are cold-blooded. All fish lay eggs, although some species store the eggs within the body, such as seahorses. Examples of fish include salmon, goldfish and sharks.
- **Reptiles** Reptiles lay eggs, are cold-blooded and usually have four limbs. They have dry, scaly skin and lay leathery eggs on land, even if they live in water. Examples of reptiles include crocodiles, snakes and turtles.
- **Amphibians** Amphibians have slimy skin, lay jelly-like eggs, are cold-blooded and have four limbs. They are able to breathe both on land and underwater. Amphibians lay eggs in water. Examples of amphibians include frogs, toads and salamanders.

A quick note when talking about 'warm-blooded' and 'cold-blooded' animals. Strictly, these are not very useful terms. Most animals are unable to regulate their body temperature, so their body temperature is whatever their local environment is. They are known as **poikilotherms**. However, birds and mammals are able to generate their own heat and maintain their body temperature independent of the surrounding temperature. They are called **homeotherms**.

Comparing similar animals

Think about a great white shark and an orca. In what ways are they the same? In what ways are they different?

Whales may be wrongly classified as fish since they look very similar to sharks. A whale is a mammal, while a shark is a fish. Whales are warm-blooded and they give birth to live young which they feed with milk. They have lungs and so cannot breathe underwater, coming to the surface to breathe.

Sharks are cold-blooded and can breathe underwater using gills. They lay eggs. Many sharks hold the eggs inside their body until they hatch, but there is no placenta and they do not suckle the babies with milk.

Classification in more detail

In Year 6, pupils look more closely at Linnean classification, in which living creatures can be classified into kingdoms. They should be introduced to the idea that these broad groupings, such as micro-organisms, plants and animals, can be subdivided. This continues from the work done in Year 4.

All living creatures can be divided into five **kingdoms**, based on certain characteristics, the most important characteristic being what their cells look like.

The three main kingdoms to consider at primary level are:

- **Animals** Any organism made of more than one cell that feeds on plants or other animals.
- **Plants** A living organism that is able to make its own food by the process of photosynthesis. Plants are made of more than one cell with specialist tissues.
- **Fungi** A group of organisms that include microorganisms like yeast and moulds. Fungi play an important role in decomposing plant and animal matter. Examples of fungi include athlete's foot, ringworm, mushrooms and toadstools.

As a simple rule, if it's green, has specialist parts and can make its own food using sunlight, then it's a plant. If it can move around and eats other living things, then it's an animal. Fungi cannot make their own food and mainly eat dead and decaying animal and plant material.

In addition to these three kingdoms, there are also two more, but these may be best left until KS3:

- **Protists** A group of organisms that either have one cell or many cells, but no specialist tissues. Protists include amoeba, protozoa, seaweeds and some algae.
- **Monera** Simple, single-celled microscopic organisms without a nucleus. Monera include **bacteria** and blue-green algae.

Instead of these two kingdoms, primary-age children could consider just 'microorganisms' as a group, including bacteria, amoeba and protozoa. These are simple living things, made of only one cell, which you can only see with a microscope.

Dividing further

The modern classification system was started by Carl Linnaeus in the eighteenth century. He originally only classified things as animals or plants, with other kingdoms coming later as we learnt more about the natural world.

Linnaeus proposed placing living things into progressively smaller and smaller groups. These are: kingdom, phylum, class, order, family, genus and species.

So, for us as human beings, our classification would look like:

- Kingdom: Animal
- Phylum: Vertebrate
- Class: Mammal
- Order: Primate
- Family: Hominid
- Genus: Homo
- Species: *Homo sapiens*

Because of Linnaeus, all living things have a two-part name, which we call the binomial system. This comprises a genus name followed by a specific (species) name. So, for the big cats, such as lions and tigers, the genus name is Panthera. A lion would be *Panthera leo* and a tiger would be *Panthera tigris*.

Classification and keys

Classification keys are a tool for identifying an unknown organism based on distinct features. They involve answering a series of questions about the organism's physical characteristics. The answers will branch off to other questions and eventually identify the organism.

The working scientifically requirements for Lower KS2 children require them to be able to make use of ready-made keys. In Upper KS2, they should be able to use and develop their own keys.

When making a key, it is important to remind the pupils that the questions must be answerable with a 'yes' or a 'no'. So, you could ask 'Does it have six legs?', but you shouldn't ask 'How many legs does it have?'.

Tip

Demonstrate how to make a key by mapping it out on the floor using sheets of A4 paper with arrows on them. Use other sheets for the questions. Children can then physically move through the key. Stopping on a question and following either the 'yes' or 'no' arrow to the next question. You might need to do this in the hall as the keys can get quite large!

Branching databases

Creating keys provides an opportunity for some cross-curricular links to computing and maths. Check your school computers for any software that can be used to create branching databases such as Purple Mash or J2E Branch. These can be used to create identification keys for different living things.

Habitats

Planet Earth is our home and we need to look after it and all the animals and plants that live in it. A full understanding of habitats and ecosystems allows us to appreciate how we can manage them and conserve the resources within them. Children begin to learn about this in Year 2 when they should be introduced to the terms 'habitat' and 'micro-habitat'.

A **habitat** is any part of the environment in which a community of organisms is found. A habitat must provide food, water, air (oxygen for respiration in all living things and carbon dioxide for photosynthesis in plants), warmth/shelter, light and a place to reproduce.

A habitat may be as small as a single leaf or rock, or as large as a rainforest or the ocean, depending on the organisms that live within it. There may be competition between the organisms in a habitat for the limited resources, but also some interdependence of the species that live there.

A **microhabitat** is a very small habitat, forming part of a much larger habitat – for example, underneath stones and logs in a woodland, or under the soil.

Read more about food chains in Chapter 6.

Hunting for minibeasts

The various invertebrates that are found in any school grounds are often known as **minibeasts** – these include insects, spiders, snails and small crustaceans such as woodlice. It is a common activity to collect and classify examples of these animals. The children can do this in a simple way in KS1, and then with a little more depth in Year 4.

Simple equipment, such as soft brushes, pooters, hand lenses and clear containers with lids containing air holes, can be used to collect and study the minibeasts in greater detail, helping the children to become immersed in their environment. Have some simple identification keys on hand for the children to use to identify any animals found. Shake a branch of a tree over a white sheet placed on the ground and see what falls off.

Ask the children to sketch or photograph the organisms they find in the different habitats they explore.

Ensure that the children take care to replace things like rocks, pots or leaves in their original positions, so that animals' habitats are not disturbed unnecessarily, as well as return all living things back to where they were found. Children should wash their hands thoroughly after the activity.

The environment at risk

In Year 4, pupils are expected to recognise that environments can change and that this can sometimes pose dangers to living things. This provides an opportunity to introduce many 'green issues' at a local and global level.

Large areas of forest are cut down each year for agriculture. These trees provide habitats for many animals.

The Great Pacific Garbage Patch is an area of plastic debris in the North Pacific Ocean covering an area of 20 million square kilometres.

Children will be aware of climate change and some of the problems due to pollution. Use books such as *Greta and the Giants* (Tucker, 2019) to introduce these ideas.

Sustainability links

There are plenty of opportunities to link this topic area to different sustainability goals. The children could suggest different ways to improve their school's environmental footprint, such as biodiversity. They could look at the biodiversity around the school grounds and suggest ways to improve with wildflower areas, insect houses, etc.

They could find out about palm oil and how rainforests are being cut down in places such as Indonesia and Malaysia to grow it, which harms animals such as orangutans. They could research how rising global temperatures are affecting polar bears or causing bleaching of coral reefs.

Animal life cycles

All living creatures go through a series of developmental stages known as a life cycle. For most plants and animals, the cycle begins when an ovum (egg cell) is fertilised by a sperm (male sex cell). As the organism's cells multiply, it grows and matures into adulthood. At this point, the organism is able to reproduce and the cycle continues with the next generation. In something like a chicken, the life cycle looks like this.

Pupils often think of an egg as the 'start' of a life cycle. In fact, since the different stages repeat in a continuous cycle, there is technically no point at which you should start. However, it could be said that each individual organism starts life as a fertilised egg.

The answer to the old question – what came first, the chicken or the egg? – is quite clearly the egg, as animals such as fish, amphibians and reptiles were laying eggs long before there were chickens!

There is a wide range of life cycles you can study, and, if you like, you can include great examples of different models for parental care such as midwife toads and seahorses or total lack of care such as coral or sea anemones.

Metamorphosis

For most animals, the juvenile form looks just like a smaller version of the adult, but this is not for every animal. For animals such as amphibians and insects, the juveniles look totally different from the adults. They then undergo a process called **metamorphosis** in which they undergo a significant transformation to become an adult.

For amphibians, this means growing legs, developing lungs and losing their gills. A tadpole therefore gradually changes into a frog.

For insects, the changes can alter their entire body, including growing legs, wings, eyes and antennae. A caterpillar will spin a cocoon and then emerge as a butterfly.

Observing life cycles

One of the challenges in teaching this topic area is that most life cycles take place over a long period of time, so they can't always be observed in the classroom.

However, it may be possible to show the pupils some examples of different life-cycle stages as a series of images or as time-lapse videos.

Some zoos and wildlife parks place webcams in nest boxes or enclosures so that visitors can watch the babies. If you have a school pond, it may be possible to carefully observe frogspawn and tadpoles in the spring. Caterpillars can be bought online and delivered in the post, allowing pupils to observe the life-cycle stages from caterpillar to butterfly over a few weeks. Some companies loan out incubators and eggs to observe chicks hatching and then find homes for the chickens once grown. Search for 'ethical chick hatching' to find reputable companies that do this.

How does a caterpillar turn into a butterfly?

After hatching from its egg, a butterfly spends the first part of its life as a caterpillar. This is the butterfly's larval stage. The caterpillar is an eating machine, getting bigger and bigger.

The caterpillar then enters what is known as the pupa stage. It hangs upside down from a twig or leaf and sheds its skin to reveal a hard protective casing called a chrysalis.

Amazing changes happen inside the chrysalis. The caterpillar releases special enzymes that break down almost all of its tissues, essentially forming a caterpillar soup of cells. Special groups of cells then begin to build all the adult body parts, such as legs, wings, eyes and antennae. Once it has rebuilt its body, the adult butterfly emerges from the chrysalis.

Asexual reproduction in plants

Living things are able to **reproduce** in two different ways – **sexual reproduction** and **asexual reproduction**.

In plants, sexual reproduction involves pollen from one flower fertilising the egg of another to produce a seed. This is covered in Year 3 plants.

To read more on this, see Chapter 4.

In Year 5, children should also learn that plants are capable of reproducing asexually. In asexual reproduction, only one parent is needed and the offspring are genetically identical clones of the parent. Some plants, like potatoes, produce tubers. These sit under the soil and develop into new plants the next year. Some plants, like strawberries, grow runners that give rise to new plants. Other plants produce bulbs, like daffodils and tulips, which can split to create more bulbs.

You can also take cuttings of plants. It is possible to take just a leaf from a plant, such as geranium or a short stem of rosemary, add some rooting powder and plant it in a pot, and it will grow roots and become a whole new plant.

Sex and fertilisation

Within primary science, you should only cover fertilisation in animals at the level of 'sperm plus egg equals baby'. Reproduction in humans, including sex and relationships, should be kept to Relationships and Sex Education (RSE or PSHE) lessons, and parents are usually notified about this. Ask in your school about their sex education policy.

It is not necessary for the pupils to understand about genes or DNA. Explain that an egg and a sperm each contains half of the information needed to make a new living thing. When a sperm meets and joins with an egg, there is enough information to produce offspring. The egg and sperm then start to grow and develop into the animal.

Challenges and misconceptions the children may have

Pupils sometimes find it difficult to distinguish between homes and habitats. It might help to explain to them that a 'home' is a place of shelter for an organism where it might spend some time. A habitat must provide all the requirements for life to keep the organism alive.

Children may consider a habitat as something that is static and unchanging, whereas most habitats change considerably over time due to human activity, changes in climate and seasonal variations.

Children often think that ecosystems are simply a collection of animals and plants living independently. In fact, everything interconnects, with each living thing relying on others for survival. You could start to discuss this with the children by examining an individual animal they are familiar with, and begin to look at the other animals and plants it interacts with. Asking questions helps to prompt discussion, such as what does the animal eat? What eats it? What happens to its waste products?

Making the learning real: linking the unit to everyday life

You can relate this topic to real-world examples that the children would have experienced in order to embed these concepts. Children could consider their pets or other animals they see every day. Ask them to think about where they like to live and what kinds of food they eat. If any children have exotic pets, such as snakes or lizards, describe the special arrangements that they need to look after them. Do they live in a bare cage or tank? What sorts of things do they add to the enclosure to enrich the environment for their pet?

You could link this topic to a trip to the zoo. Children could think about the different ways that the zookeepers create a more natural habitat for the animals. If you can't visit a zoo, you could find video clips online of life behind-the-scenes life at a zoo.

By upper primary, children should already have an understanding of their own environment. They may already be aware of local problems such as pollution and litter, and possible global problems too, such as climate change or major oil disasters.

Practical lesson ideas

Classification keys

Play '20 questions' in pairs or as a class. One child thinks of an object and the other child has to ask questions which can only have a yes or no answer to guess what the object is. The board game 'Guess Who?' is also a great way to introduce this idea. You could play something similar with the whole class. Everybody stands up and then they sit down if they don't have the characteristic the teacher describes – ponytail, glasses, brown hair, etc.

Who lives where?

Match photographs of different habitats to photographs of different animals and plants that might live there. Pupils should compare animals in familiar habitats with animals found in less familiar habitats – for example, on the seashore, in woodland, in the ocean, in the rainforest.

Build a bug hotel

A simple bug hotel could be made from a small pile of hollow stems or bamboo, bound together. A grander one could be made from several wooden pallets layered on top of each other with twigs, leaves, straw plastic pipes and bricks filling the holes.

Cross-curricular links and opportunities

In KS1

This topic area provides many storytelling opportunities about different animals and where they live. A story such as *The Gruffalo* (Donaldson, 1999) provides a fun starting-point for discussing how a deep, dark wood can be a habitat for many different animals. The children could find out about some of the stories from different cultures – for example, the Anansi stories of African folk tales.

There are plenty of opportunities to link with Art and Design and Technology. The children could paint pictures inspired by different types of habitat or make collages of pictures of animals and plants that live in the same habitat.

In geography, the children could find out about different habitats around the world, such as deserts, rainforests and coral reefs.

In KS2

This topic has many links with geography through looking at global environmental issues such as pollution, climate change and human impact on the environment. Discussion about local and global environmental issues can also form part of personal and social education or citizenship lessons.

In literacy, children could write poems or songs about animals living in different habitats, or about environmental issues. They can produce presentations about endangered animals or the importance of recycling. They could produce information campaigns using posters, leaflets and even short films or podcasts.

In maths, the children could produce graphs and charts to compare data from different habitats over a year, such as average temperature or rainfall. Dataloggers or thermometers could be used to collect local temperature data over the course of a week or month.

Progression

The study of living things begins with a look at habitats and simple food chains. It looks at what makes something alive, then how we classify animals and plants. It then looks at life cycles and the processes of reproduction.

There is a lot of overlap between the Living Things and Habitats and the Animals Including Humans units, so consider both units when tracking how progression occurs through the years.

Suggested scientists

There are a great many conservationists and naturalists who could be featured here that children might like to research. Some examples include:

- **Liz Bonnin** Irish science, wildlife and natural history presenter. Works on big cat conservation programmes for the Zoological Society of London.
- **Eunice Newton Foote** The first person to publish a scientific paper on climate change, showing the link between carbon dioxide and atmospheric warming.
- **Rachel Carson** American biologist who wrote about the dangers of environmental pollution.
- **Paula Kahumbu** Wildlife conservationist, particularly involved in protecting elephants.

Further reading and resources

Nicholson, D. (2020) 'Keys and classification using finger puppets': www.science-fix.co.uk/2020/11/keys-and-classification-using-finger-puppets/

RHS 'Minibeast identification key': https://schoolgardening.rhs.org.uk/resources/info-sheet/mini-beast-identification-key

RSC 'Sustainability contexts for primary science': https://edu.rsc.org/primary-science/sustainability-contexts-for-primary-science/4014614.article

Teaching about puberty: https://healthyschoolscp.org.uk/pshe/puberty

WWF 'Schools sustainability guide': www.wwf.org.uk/get-involved/schools/sustainability-guide

Young People's Trust for the Environment: 'Minibeasts': https://ypte.org.uk/factsheets/minibeasts/identifying-minibeasts

CHAPTER 6

Animals, including Humans

Introduction

It is natural to have a curiosity about our own body and how it works. For thousands of years, humans have worked to unravel the mysteries of the human body and how to fix it when it goes wrong. An understanding of how the body works is very important in keeping ourselves fit and healthy, and even today there is still much we don't know about diseases such as dementia and cancer, and how best to treat them.

By incorporating animal and human biology into our teaching, we can inspire children's curiosity, foster empathy and help them develop a deeper understanding of the natural world.

Science knowledge you need before you can teach this topic

Identify and name a variety of common animals

Young children will experience a range of different animals while out and about with their family, on trips to the park and the zoo, and through films, television and in story books. Children are able to name more examples of vertebrates such as mammals and birds than invertebrates (Patrick and Tunnicliffe, 2011).

Provide plenty of opportunities for the children to see a wide variety of animals through images, stories and videos throughout their time in school.

Carnivores, herbivores and omnivores

Unlike plants, animals are unable to make their own food and must rely on the food that has been made by plants. Some animals do this by eating plants; some do it by eating other animals; and some do both.

- **Herbivores** Animals that eat only plants. They have specially adapted digestive systems that are well suited to digesting plant matter. Common herbivores include guinea pigs, rabbits and squirrels. Farm animals such as sheep, cows and goats are herbivores.
- **Carnivores** Animals that eat only meat. They are especially adapted for catching, killing and digesting other animals. Common carnivores include cats, spiders and frogs, owls and kestrels.
- **Omnivores** These animals have a diet that consists of both meat and plant material. Omnivores include badgers, hedgehogs and foxes. Many garden birds, like robins, sparrows and blackbirds, will eat fruit and berries, but will also eat insects and worms. Most pet dogs are also omnivores, mixing meat with grains and other plants.

In Key Stage 1, pupils should consider what foods different animals need to stay alive. They could link this to different pets they might have at home – you wouldn't give cat food to a guinea pig, for example.

The basic structure of animals

In KS1, the children should be able to describe and compare the structure of a variety of different animals. As with animal diets above, a good starting point would be to think about pets at home, and then expand this to look at other common animals they might also be aware of. Use videos and photographs as examples. Real examples too are always great if you have a class pet or can arrange a visit to a farm or a zoo.

- **Fish** have gills to breathe underwater. They have fins and a tail that help to propel them through the water. Most fish have scales.
- **Amphibians** have four legs instead of fins. They usually have webbed feet to help them to swim. Some amphibians, such as newts, still have a tail but frogs and toads do not. They don't have gills and can't breathe underwater.

- **Reptiles** look very similar to amphibians in that they have four legs and a tail, but reptiles are dry and scaly. Aquatic reptiles have webbed feet.
- **Birds** have two legs. They also have wings (which are modified front legs). Birds have a hard beak and are covered in feathers.

Basic parts of the human body

KS1 children should be able to point to and name the basic external parts of the human body. This will include arms, legs, fingers, elbows, knees and neck. It will also include eyes, ears, the mouth and nose. Obviously, songs such as 'Head, Shoulders, Knees and Toes' or 'One Finger, One Thumb, Keep Moving' can be used to good effect here.

The different body parts can also be linked to the senses; eyes to sight, ears to sound, mouth (and tongue) to taste, fingers to touch and nose to smell. Provide practical opportunities for the children to explore these different senses with objects to feel, things to taste and smell, etc.

The basic needs of animals and humans

You can find animals living just about anywhere on Earth, even in the coldest habitats of the Arctic and Antarctic. Humans can even live above the Earth in spacecraft such as the International Space Station. But no matter where we live, there are some things that humans and all other animals cannot survive without. We call these things our basic needs. These are: food, water, oxygen and shelter.

Food gives us energy, as well as many other nutrients our bodies need to stay healthy

Different animals need different types and amounts of food. Most humans eat every few hours, while some snakes won't eat for weeks after consuming a large meal. We store excess food as fat, then break it down if food is scarce.

Water is needed for our bodies to function properly

Our bodies are made of roughly 50–70 per cent water. We lose water through our urine and sweat, so we need to top it up regularly. A supply of water is vital – our bodies can only survive a few days without it.

Oxygen is needed to get the energy out of our food and make our bodies work

Animals living on land get oxygen from air, while aquatic animals such as fish and octopuses have gills to absorb oxygen from water. Some simple animals such as jellyfish can absorb the oxygen directly from the water. KS1 children won't need to know this, but this process is called **respiration** and it takes place inside every cell of our bodies.

Shelter protects us from the environment

A good animal home protects them from harsh weather, keeping them warm at night or cool during the day. It also protects them from predators. Animals such as birds build nests. Some animals dig underground burrows to sleep in.

Survival experts refer to the 'rule of 3'. We can survive for three minutes without oxygen, three days without water and three weeks without food.

Food and nutrition

A common misconception is that we only need to eat food to give us energy (Allen, 2019). As well as the chemicals that give us energy, our food also provides us with other nutrients and chemicals that our bodies need to function properly, such as fats, proteins, vitamins and minerals.

The food that we eat can be divided into different groups. There are a few different ways of doing this, but one way to classify the different food groups is as follows.

Table 6.1 Food groups

Group	Used for	Examples
Starchy foods (carbohydrates)	Energy	Bread, potatoes, pasta, rice
Milk and dairy	Calcium for strong bones and teeth	Milk, cheese, yoghurt
Fat and sugar	Energy	Chocolate, fizzy drinks
Protein	Growth, building muscles	Fish, eggs, meat, beans, pulses
Fruit and vegetables	Vitamins, minerals and fibre	Apples, carrots, bananas

It is important when talking to children that we don't label certain foods as being 'healthy' or 'unhealthy'. Instead, discuss what makes up a balanced diet, with a good combination of all different food groups. Lettuce is seen as a healthy food, but if that is all you eat, then you will become ill with malnutrition. You can use *The Eatwell Guide* produced by Public Health England as an example of a balanced diet.

Avoid asking children to make and analyse a food diary, as this can lead to problems with children in food poverty or with eating disorders. It is better to provide them with a diary of a fictional character, perhaps from a book you are reading as a class. Pupils could carry out a survey of the meals served in the school canteen over a typical week: how balanced is it overall?

Sustainability links

Look at the food miles of the food we eat. How much food do we waste and how could we manage that better? Consider plant-based diets.

The skeleton, muscles and movement

Bones are very important to us – without our skeleton, we wouldn't be able to do much at all.

All vertebrates, including humans, have a skeleton inside their bodies. This performs three very important roles:

- **Support** Our skeleton gives the body its structure and allows us to stand upright. It provides a frame for all our organs to hang from.
- **Protection** Some of our most important organs are protected by bones. The skull encases our soft, delicate brain and protects it from damage. Our ribs form a protective cage to protect the heart and lungs.
- **Movement** Bones have muscles attached to them. The muscles make the bones move by pulling on them, which in turn allows us to move around.

Muscles can only pull, they cannot push. A muscle contracts and gets shorter, which will pull on the bone and make it move. Muscles usually work in pairs – one contracts and pulls, while the other one relaxes.

There are three different types of muscle. These are:

- **Voluntary** These move bones at joints. We are in direct control of them and can move them whenever we want to. They are strong muscles, but they can get tired easily.
- **Involuntary** These muscles work automatically without having to think about it. Examples include the muscles that push food down our oesophagus when we swallow, move food through our intestines or open/close blood vessels.
- **Cardiac** These muscles are only found in the heart and make the heart beat. They are very strong and can work constantly without getting tired. They contract automatically.

A **joint** is a place where two or more bones meet. This is usually somewhere obvious like a knee or elbow, but there are also joints between the bones in our spine and in our skull. There are many different types of joint that the pupils should be aware of: ball and socket (like the shoulder), hinge (like the knee), and immovable joints like those between the bones in our skull.

Tendons connects muscles to bones. Tendons work together with muscles to enable movement of the skeleton.

Ligaments connect bones together at joints. Ligaments protect joints by keeping them stable and restricting movement.

Teeth

Typically, our mouth contains several different types of teeth, each with a different role. These are:

- **Incisors** The teeth at the front of our mouth. Humans have four on the top row of teeth and four on the bottom row. Incisors are used for biting into, cutting and chopping food.
- **Canines** The pointed teeth at the front of the mouth, either side of the incisors. Canine teeth help rip and tear food.
- **Molars** The wide flat teeth at the back of our mouth. These are used for grinding food.

Ask the children to think about what teeth they use when eating their food. When taking a bite, they will use their incisors and canines. When nibbling at something, they might only use their incisors. When chewing, they will move their food to the back of their mouth and use their molars.

Herbivore vs. carnivore teeth

Because of the different foods they chew on, herbivore teeth have adapted differently to carnivore teeth. Pupils should look at a variety of different examples to compare how their teeth look.

In a carnivore such as a cat or a dog, the teeth have adapted to a life of eating meat. The molars at the back of the mouth are very sharp and slide over each other like a pair of scissors. This is ideal for ripping and cutting meat. Large canine teeth at the front help when biting and killing their prey. The incisors at the front are used in grasping prey and for tearing meat from bones.

In a herbivore such as a sheep or a cow, the teeth are very different. Plant material is very tough and needs a lot of chewing to break it up. Because of this, the back molars are wide and flat for grinding. In grass eaters such as sheep, the top set of incisors have been replaced by a flat bony plate. Often the canine teeth are missing completely.

Rodents, like rabbits, mice and hamsters, have a large pair of upper and lower incisors that never stop growing. These teeth are really good for gnawing.

Tip

You could link the topic of teeth to how scientists study dinosaur fossils to discover what they ate. Can the children be dinosaur detectives and work out if the dinosaurs were herbivores or carnivores by looking at the teeth? A T. Rex had curved teeth the size of bananas!

Internal organs

Children often find it hard to make connections between the different organs, drawing them as isolated circles. The heart is often drawn as a Valentine's heart (Andersson et al., 2020; Reiss and Tunnicliffe, 2001). The brain is frequently depicted as a simple round shape in the head region. Lungs are crude round shapes on either side of the body. Intestines are drawn as wavy lines or tubes coming from the stomach area downwards.

Tip

Use ICT tools to visualise inside the body. A great tool to use is the website ZygoteBody which provides an interactive map of the human body. It is brilliant for exploring systems such as the heart/lungs or the skeleton. There are also interesting augmented-reality apps such as Curiscope (which works by superimposing the organs over a special T-shirt). It enables you to peer inside the body and see the heart beating, really providing the 'wow' factor when used with a class.

Details of both these resources can be found in the Further reading and resources section at the end of this chapter.

What is digestion?

The chemicals in our food are too large for our bodies to use. **Digestion** is the process by which our bodies break the food down into very small pieces – pieces that are so small that we would need a microscope to see them. Special chemicals, called enzymes, work a bit like a pair of scissors. They chop up the long chemicals into much smaller pieces. These small chemicals can then be absorbed into the body and used to make other chemicals.

Tip

You can model this with a length of string. Use a pair of scissors and chop the string up into smaller pieces.

The digestive system

Digestion is a complex body system with a number of components. Although pupils do not need to know all the details of digestion, they should be familiar with the basic organs and the order that food passes through them.

The main parts of the digestive system are:

- **Stomach** Food is mixed with digestive juices containing acid and enzymes which start to break the big chemicals down into smaller ones.

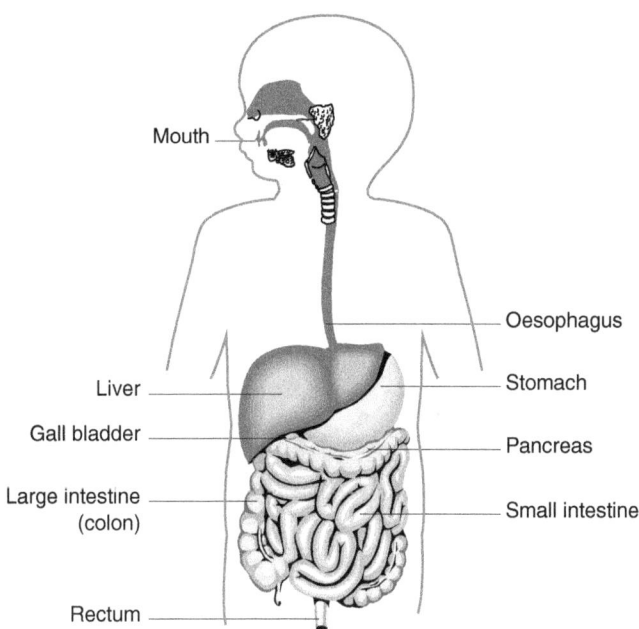

Mouth

Oesophagus

Liver

Stomach

Gall bladder

Pancreas

Large intestine
(colon)

Small intestine

Rectum

Figure 6.1   The digestive system

- **Small intestine** Nutrients, water and other useful chemicals are absorbed into blood vessels here and sent to the liver. Chemicals the body doesn't need keep passing through.
- **Liver** The nutrients absorbed from the small intestine are sent here. It's processed and sent to the rest of the body through the blood stream.
- **Large intestine** Water is absorbed and other waste products produced by the body are added as it passes through.
- **Rectum** Waste stays here and then leaves the body as poo when we go to the toilet.

You don't need to cover things like the gall bladder or pancreas, but it might come up in discussion, particularly if any pupils are diabetic or know someone with a digestive problem.

Digestion is an important process and it's fun to be able to explore how it works. You could introduce scientists who studied digestion in rather gross ways like Lazzarro Spallanzani who would swallow food on a string and regurgitate it, or William Beaumont who studied a man who had been shot in the stomach, putting food through the hole, then pulling it out later to see what had happened to it.

Food chains

To show the feeding relationships between organisms in an ecosystem, we can draw a food chain. Although it is called a food chain, it is actually showing the flow of energy from one organism to the next. The flow of energy is represented by arrows in a diagram.

A simple food chain might look like Figure 6.2.

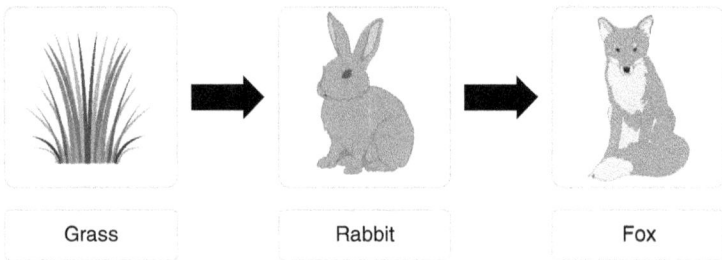

| Grass | Rabbit | Fox |

Figure 6.2   A simple food chain

Source: Images sourced from rawpixel.com

Every food chain consists of both producers and consumers.

Producers are (nearly always) plants that make their own food through photo-synthesis.

Consumers are animals that obtain energy by eating plants or other animals that have eaten plants. Pupils often get confused with the arrows in a food chain. Many think that the arrow in the food chain means 'eats' and draw the arrows in the wrong direction.

Take another look at the food chain above. Each arrow represents the flow of energy from the plant to the rabbit to the fox. The pupils could think of it as showing that the grass 'goes into' the rabbit and then the rabbit 'goes into' the fox.

Print out photographs of the fox, rabbit and grass along with large arrows and create food chains running on the floor for the children to explore. Explain what's happening as they walk along it.

Sometimes, the situation is more complicated than that shown in a food chain. The top carnivore eats more than one food, for instance. This is why a food web is a better way to represent the relationships in an ecosystem, but this is something to look at in KS3.

Animals that eat other animals are called predators, and the animals they eat are called prey. Children could look at the differences in the way that predators and prey look – in what way does a lion look different from an antelope, for example?

Sustainability link

Explore food chains in different habitats such as rainforests, the Arctic and coral reefs. Discuss how the different organisms rely on each other. Use this to discuss the dangers that different habitats face.

Human life cycles

In Year 5, the entire unit is devoted to considering the changes that take place as humans develop from babies to old age. This needs to be handled sensitively, particularly the discussion of adolescence. There are obvious links to be made to Life Cycles in the Living Things and Habitats unit.

This is a really important unit to cover. In order to keep children safe, it is essential that they learn about puberty before it happens to them (Family Planning Association). Ideally, children should be taught about puberty in UKS2, which should be just before children start to go through it themselves. This helps them prepare and informs them of the changes their body will experience.

The stages of the human life cycle are:

- Foetus
- Baby
- Childhood
- Adolescent
- Adult
- Old age.

Each stage has particular characteristics. Children can identify differences and features of each stage.

Explain that puberty usually starts between the ages of 8 and 14 and lasts for up to four years. Children will start puberty at different times. Girls usually start earlier than boys.

Puberty forms part of the science curriculum and as such is statutory content, which means that it must be taught in schools. This is unlike sex education, which parents can choose to withdraw their children from. The changes that occur during puberty, as well as the process of fertilisation, are therefore something that needs to be taught as part of science. Teaching about sex and relationships falls under PSHE (Personal, Social, Health and Economic) education. It would be useful to liaise with the school PSHE coordinator to make sure this is covered properly.

There are opportunities to link the topic of human development to other subject areas such as religious education. Many religions have 'coming of age' ceremonies at particular milestones in a child's life, such as First Holy Communion and Confirmation, or Bar and Bat Mitzvahs.

The heart and circulatory system

The heart is the pump that powers everything you do. Whether you're sleeping or running a marathon, the constant beat of your heart keeps you alive.

Your heart is a muscle whose only function is to pump blood around the body. It is about the size of your fist and is located slightly to the left of the centre of your chest, not over on the far left as some people think. It is also not shaped like a Valentine's heart, as many children think.

The heart has two sides and each side has two chambers, the atrium and ventricle. The blood enters the heart into the **atria**, then flows into the **ventricles** where it is then pumped out.

The right side of the heart receives blood from the body and pumps it to the lungs where it picks up oxygen. The left side receives the oxygen-rich blood from the lungs and pumps it from the left ventricle out to the body via the aorta.

- The blood vessels that carry blood away from the heart are called **arteries**.
- The blood vessels that carry blood back to the heart are called **veins**.
- The tiny blood vessels inside muscles and organs are called **capillaries**.

Remember: **a**rtery = **a**way (from the heart).

As the blood moves out of the heart, the arteries carry blood to all the different parts of the body, delivering oxygen and 'fuel' powering everything from your brain to your muscles.

Blood is kept flowing in one direction by flaps of tissue in the heart, called **valves**. It is the closing of these valves that makes the characteristic lub-dub sound of a heartbeat.

Tip

Pupils could role-play the movement of blood around the body in the playground or in the hall. A small group of children at one end act as the body and a group at the other end are the lungs, with a small group in-between acting as the heart. Pupils move in a figure of eight, from the body, through the heart to the lungs, and back again. They could even carry tokens to represent oxygen which they collect at the lungs and deliver to the body, collecting a carbon dioxide token to bring back to the lungs.

What is blood?

Blood is not just a liquid; it is made of four different components.

- **Red blood cells** These tiny, round cells deliver oxygen around your body. They are packed with a protein called haemoglobin, which is able to join with oxygen and transport it.
- **White blood cells** These cells patrol your bloodstream and fight infection. Some will engulf any foreign bodies such as bacteria and viruses, while others produce chemicals to help kill them. They are an important part of our immune system.
- **Platelets** These small cell fragments are vital to repair damage to your body. When you get a cut, platelets clump together at the site of the damage and form a clot that stops the bleeding.
- **Plasma** This is the liquid part of the blood in which all the other blood components float. The plasma helps transport nutrients and hormones. It also transports waste products around the body such as urea to the kidneys and carbon dioxide to the lungs.

Effect of exercise

Every cell in your body carries out a process called **respiration** in order to release the energy it needs to function. Aerobic respiration requires oxygen and produces carbon dioxide as a waste product. We need to breathe in and out in order to get oxygen into our blood and the carbon dioxide out.

As your body exercises, your muscles are respiring more because they need more energy. This means they require more oxygen as well as producing more carbon dioxide.

Your breathing rate will increase to get more oxygen into the blood and to remove more carbon dioxide. At the same time, the heart will pump faster to deliver more oxygen to the muscles and remove the carbon dioxide and get it back to the lungs.

Respiration can also occur in the absence of oxygen. This is called anaerobic respiration. Anaerobic respiration is less efficient than aerobic respiration and can only be used for short periods at a time. It produces lactic acid, which, if allowed to build up, can cause cramp. This is why runners might get cramp or a stitch when running as the lactic acid builds up.

After exercise, it takes a while for the body to recover, until the demand for extra energy falls and any lactic acid is removed. Eventually, the heart rate and breathing returns to normal.

Sustainability link

How can we encourage children to exercise and stay active to keep healthy as they grow up?

How are nutrients and water transported within animals?

In humans, water and nutrients are transported around the body by the heart and blood vessels, as described above. Humans have a double loop, with blood going from the heart to the lungs, back to the heart then off to the body. Blood is carried inside blood vessels, which is called a closed system.

Other animals do it differently. For example, fish have gills instead of lungs. Blood flows from the heart to the gills where they pick up oxygen and dump carbon dioxide. Blood then flows to the body to drop off the oxygen and pick up carbon dioxide. Blood then flows back to the heart. There's only a single loop.

Sustainability link

Look at the importance of clean water and the need to conserve and protect our fresh water supplies.

Effect of diet, drugs and lifestyle on the body

Our lifestyle choices can have a major impact on our health and well-being. Children should understand the risks of various factors such as unhealthy diets, harmful substances and a lack of exercise.

Harmful substances to discuss include tobacco, alcohol, solvents and other recreational drugs.

A drug is any chemical that can alter how different parts of the body works, including the brain. Many medicines are also drugs and need to be treated carefully. Not all drugs are medicines. Coordinate with your PSHE lead.

Sustainability link

Explore healthy living and promote well-being. Think about dietary issues faced by poor and vulnerable people around the world and the impact of malnutrition.

Challenges and misconceptions the children may have

Pupils develop many different ideas about the bones and muscles in their bodies. They will probably be aware of the muscles in their arms and legs, as they use these often, but they might not realise that muscles are found all around the body. Ask them to think about how our eyes move or how our mouth changes shape.

Pupils may not realise that bones are actually living tissue (Caravita and Falchetti, 2005). They may know that milk is good for their bones and teeth, but may not know that this is because it contains lots of calcium, a mineral needed for building and maintaining healthy bones and teeth.

It is commonly believed, even by adults, that arterial blood is red and venous blood is blue. This is a really hard misconception to dispel, and not helped by every textbook diagram showing blood as red and blue. Many believe that the reason why we don't see blue blood when we cut ourselves is because it becomes red as soon as it contacts the air (Allen, 2019). This is not true. While it is true that your veins look blue when you look at them, this is due to the way they scatter and absorb red and blue light. The vein might look blue, but the blood inside is still a dark red colour.

Making the learning real: Linking the unit to everyday life

The benefit of teaching a topic like the human body is that everybody in the class will have one. Teaching about bones and muscles can immediately be explored by just moving your arm or your fingers and observing different muscles changing size and tendons flexing. You can feel your heart beating and your lungs inflating and deflating.

When discussing animals and the needs of animals, many children will have pets and will know that the pets need to be looked after to stay healthy. They will know the kinds of food their pets eat, which could lead into a discussion about herbivores and carnivores. They might be able to discuss why you wouldn't feed dog food to a rabbit.

Children will already have heard varying advice on how to stay healthy from their parents or from TV and YouTube. They might have already been told that sugary foods are bad for their teeth or that too much chocolate might make them fat. Use these ideas as a starting point to discuss healthy diets.

Some of the children in your class might have younger siblings who they have seen grow and develop from babies to toddlers. They may also have seen baby photographs of themselves, so will be able to describe some of the ways in which they have changed. Or they may have elderly relatives and can describe some of the changes associated with getting old. As has already been discussed, puberty will be something that is relevant to all Year 5 children as a change they will be going through soon.

Practical lesson ideas

Stacking food chains

Give each group of pupils several plastic or cardboard drinking cups. Ask them to draw individual animals and plants, then cut out and stick one animal or plant onto the side of each upside-down cup. Write the name of the organism around the lip of the cup so that it can be seen when the cups are stacked. Stack the cups in different combinations to make different food chains. Take photographs of each combination as a record.

Effect of acid on teeth

A classic investigation is to look at the effect of acids on teeth, using clean eggshells as a stand-in for real teeth. You can use vinegar, orange juice, cola and water as a control. Leave the shells in the liquids for a few days. Change the liquid often as it can become rather smelly.

Modelling the process of digestion

One of my favourite demonstrations is to make a model of the digestive system using a plastic bag, paper cups and a pair of tights to see what happens to a cream cracker and a banana (see the Further reading and resources section at end of the chapter for more information and instructions).

Who's poo is this?

Ask the children to look at different types of poo (no, really). You could make herbivore, carnivore and omnivore poo in advance from Play-Doh. Add grass and seeds for herbivore poo and bits of dry pasta for carnivore poo (to stand in for bones). See if they can work out which is which. You could link this to books such as *The Story of the Little Mole Who Knew it Was None of His Business* (Holzwarth, 2019) or *Poo in the Zoo* (Smallman, 2015). Can the pupils identify what animal made the poo? For a good fake poo recipe, see the YAC link in the Further reading and resources section at the end of the chapter.

Exploring bones

Provide the pupils with opportunities to handle real bones where possible. Left-over chicken bones from meals can be cleaned by boiling them for 40 minutes, then allowing them to cool. Scrub off any excess meat then sterilise it with disinfectant. Leave it to dry before use.

In an investigation, the pupils could soak a chicken bone in different liquids for several days to see the effects. Acids like vinegar or cola will dissolve the calcium, leaving only the flexible cartilage. Use a Newton meter to see how much force is needed to bend each bone before and after soaking.

Sugar in our foods

Explore food labels of different foods and soft drinks to find out how much sugar is in a serving of each one – for example, a can of regular Coca-Cola contains 35g of sugar. Weigh out the amount of sugar using scales to see what it looks like.

Cross-curricular links and opportunities

KS1

There are opportunities for literacy and music work. The children could sing songs about the body such as 'Head, Shoulders, Knees and Toes', then make up their own versions with actions.

In art, the children could paint pictures of different animals or they could make a collage from animal pictures cut out of magazines.

KS2

There are links between how our bodies work and PE, so be sure to discuss this with your school PE lead. You could ask the children to think about what muscles are being used when taking part in different sports – for example, why does a sprinter look different from a high jumper or a shot putter? They could also listen to different musical movements from *The Carnival of the Animals* suite by Saint-Saëns such as 'Aquarium' or 'Tortoises', and think about how the music reflects how the animals move. They could create their own dances in time to the music.

There are also links to personal, social and health education when discussing the effects of exercise, smoking and drugs on the heart and lungs. This also links to puberty and adolescence.

Include literacy skills by asking children to write stories or poems related to a journey around the heart and lungs, or what it would be like to have no skeleton.

They could write scripts for an advertisement that explains how to look after your heart and lungs and stay healthy, which could be filmed or recorded as a podcast, making links to computing as well. The theme of growing up has inspired many stories and poems, some of which could be read and discussed as a class. Ask the children to write their own stories or poems about different animal life cycles. They could design storybooks for younger children, similar in style to *The Very Hungry Caterpillar* (Carle, 1969).

Progression

The children start by looking at different animals and considering their basic structure and what they eat. They then look further at different body systems such as skeletons, the digestive system and teeth. Human life cycles are explored and linked to animal life cycles. Finally, the heart and circulatory system are studied and considerations for healthy lifestyles.

There is a lot of overlap between the Living Things and Their Habitats and the Animals, Including Humans units, so consider both units when tracking how progression occurs through the years.

Suggested scientists

There are a great many anatomists and nutritionists who could be featured here that children might like to research. Some examples include:

- **John Boyd Orr** Scottish nutritionist. Campaigned for free school milk to be provided to school children in the UK in the 1930s to combat malnutrition.
- **Ibn al-Nafis** Arab physician who made significant contributions to the early knowledge of pulmonary circulation.
- **Santorio Santorio** Italian anatomist. Invented the first devices to measure heart rate and body temperature.
- **Florence Nightingale** Modernised nursing, advocated for healthcare reform and better sanitation in hospitals.
- **Elizabeth Garrett Anderson** First British female physician and surgeon.

Further reading and resources

Curiscope Virtuali-Tee: www.curiscope.co.uk/products/virtuali-tee

Family Planning Association: Teaching Puberty and the Adolescent Body: www.fpa. org.uk/guidance-teaching-puberty

'How to make blood': https://letsgolivescience.com/activity/how-to-make-blood

Live Science: (2012) 'If blood is red, why do veins look bluish?': www.livescience. com/32212-if-blood-is-red-why-are-veins-blue.html

Nicholson, D. (2019) 'Make a digestive system model using crackers and bananas': www.sciencefix.co.uk/2019/05/make-a-digestive-system-model-using-crackers-and-bananas/

PSHE Association: Teaching puberty: https://pshe-association.org.uk/resource/ changing-and-growing-up-ks2

Public Health England: The Eatwell Guide: www.food.gov.uk/business-guidance/ the-eatwell-guide-and-resources

Public Health England: Healthy Eating Teaching Resources: https://campaignresources. phe.gov.uk/schools/resources/

YAC: 'Make and excavate archaeological poo!': www.yac-uk.org/activity/make-and-excavate-archaeological-poo

Zygote Body: www.zygotebody.com

CHAPTER 7

Evolution and Inheritance

Introduction

The theory of evolution is one of the most important in biology. It reveals how all living things are related, in a family tree of life, that stretches back almost 4 billion years. Through the process of evolution living things have constantly changed and adapted to live almost everywhere on Earth.

Evolution is a controversial topic for some, but it is scientifically backed up by a wealth of scientific evidence. Evolution as a concept is fairly new to the primary national curriculum, introduced in 2014. Prior to 2014, children were taught that living things were adapted to their environment, but there was no requirement to teach the mechanism for how this adaptation occurred.

Controversial subject warning

This is a subject area that will need to be handled sensitively since evolution has become a controversial issue for members of some religious groups. Before you teach this unit, it would be worth checking your approach with your school leadership.

A belief that a God created everything that exists is shared by Christians, Jews, Muslims and many other religions all over the world. In view of this, it is important that as teachers we do not simply dismiss these traditional beliefs. On the other hand, evolution should not be treated as a belief (Williams, 2014). It is backed up by countless pieces of evidence and as such is accepted by the majority of scientists, many of whom are religious.

A belief in evolution and a belief in a God can coexist. Both Pope Francis and Pope John Paul II explained that the story of Genesis should not be taken literally and that the evidence for evolution is beyond reasonable doubt.

Some children do hold creationist beliefs and have parents who accept such views. If brought up in a science lesson, it should be handled in a way that is respectful of children's views. But, as with all misconceptions, it should be addressed with compelling evidence (Foster, 2012), clearly giving the message that the theory of evolution and the notion of an old Earth are supported by a mass of evidence (explored further later in this chapter) and fully accepted by the scientific community.

Evolution has sometimes been dismissed as 'just a theory', but this is misunderstanding the importance of a theory in science. A **theory** to a scientist means a different thing from what it does to everyone else. In everyday use, a theory means a guess or a hunch. These theories are often unproven. In science, however, a theory is a well-accepted explanation for a phenomenon based on irrefutable evidence. A theory ties together all the facts and can even be used to make predictions. Gravity is 'just' a theory, but I am sure you would think twice before jumping out of a second-floor window.

The website 'Not Just a Theory' goes into this in more detail. If you're interested in learning more, details can be found in the Further reading and resources section at the end of this chapter.

Science knowledge you need before you can teach this topic

Living things are adapted to the environment

All living things appear to be perfectly suited to life in the habitat in which you find them, whether that's a hot desert environment, a tidal rockpool or just a simple local woodland.

Think about a polar bear. What features does it have that helps it survive in the Arctic? It has a thick layer of blubber under its skin for insulation. Its fur is very thick and hollow to trap air, both of which help insulation. Its feet are large to stop it sinking into the snow, with large claws for gripping the ice and ripping apart its prey. Its white fur helps to camouflage it in the show and it has small ears to help reduce heat loss. Polar bear skin is black to absorb heat. We can say the polar bear has **adapted** to life in a very cold and snowy place like the Arctic.

Adaptations are traits that allow the organism to survive within its particular environment. These adaptations have gradually evolved by means of natural selection over a long period of time. As you introduce different animals and plants, ask the children to think about the habitats they live in, and consider the features they have that show how they are adapted for life there. Good examples to consider are animals such as camels and penguins, and plants such as a cactus.

Life has existed for a very long time

Adaptation is a slow process, but the Earth is 4.6 billion years old. The first life began in the seas around 3.6 billion years ago, which means there has been plenty of time for life to change and adapt, leading to the huge variety of life we see today.

The earliest living things were single-celled creatures such as bacteria and algae. Gradually life became more complex and multicellular life began. Plants made the move to land around 420 million years ago, and it took about 280 million years before flowers evolved. The first amphibians left the water and headed towards the land roughly 370 million years ago.

Dinosaurs ruled the Earth for 180 million years until a 10km-wide asteroid smashed into the Yucatan Peninsula in Mexico about 66 million years ago causing massive changes to the climate and the extinction of 75 per cent of all species. The death of the dinosaurs cleared the way for a small group of mammals to thrive once conditions returned to normal. They in turn evolved into primates and eventually into humans.

Human beings have existed for only a tiny fraction of the Earth's history – 200,000 years or so. If the entire history of the Earth was condensed into a 24-hour day, we wouldn't appear until a few seconds before midnight.

The table below shows a timeline for life on Earth. The timescales involved are all big numbers, and it is very hard to visualise the scale of it. You could convert the numbers into distances to produce a timeline running along a school corridor, or chalk this out on the playground.

Table 7.1   The history of life on Earth

	Million years ago
Present day	0
Modern humans appear (Homo sapiens)	0.2
Last Ice Age	2.4

(Continued)

Table 7.1 (Continued)

	Million years ago
First human-like animals appear	2.5
Dinosaurs wiped out by asteroid	66
First flowering plants	141
Birds appear	195
First dinosaurs and mammals	230
First reptiles	340
First insects	360
First amphibians	370
Plants appear on land	420
Cambrian explosion – first fish	530
Simple multicelled creatures appeared	700
Algae, fungi, single-celled animals appear	2,100
Life first begins with single-celled creatures like bacteria	3,600

Visualising deep time

Deep time refers to geological timescales that are difficult for children (and to be honest, adults) to comprehend, as they involve millions or even billions of years, since these are such huge numbers that are hard to visualise. Children may struggle to grasp just how vast these time periods are and the changes that have occurred over such long timescales. Children have a limited frame of reference and may find it challenging to connect events or phenomena from deep time to their own experiences or the world around them (App State).

Fossils show us what life used to look like

Fossils are the remains of ancient organisms preserved in rocks. By dating and sequencing these fossils, we are able to build up a picture of what lived on Earth many millions of years ago. Fossil records show a gradual change in living things, from simple to more complex forms, and they also provide evidence for intermediate forms between different groups of organisms. For example, scientists have found fossils of lizards with bird-like features, indicating that birds evolved from dinosaurs.

Children will have covered the formation of fossils in Year 3 as part of the Rocks unit. In Year 6, you can study them to provide information about living things that lived millions of years ago and how things have changed.

Children could look at images of fossils of woolly mammoths and compare them to modern elephant skeletons. They could find out about the tiktaalik, an extinct fish thought to be the ancestor of modern land animals. They could also explore some of the fossil ancestors of whales, such as *Pakicetus* and *Ambulocetus*, and compare how they changed over time.

Characteristics are passed down from parents to offspring

If you take a look at the short term, we look a lot like our parents, but if you look at inherited features over a much longer period of time, many tiny changes may have occurred, resulting in major differences when looked at over many generations (Russell and McGuigan, 2015).

Pupils will have been introduced to the idea that offspring look like their parents. They may have been told they have their father's eyes or their mother's nose, for example. It would be best to avoid dwelling too much on pointing out similarities between children and parents, as they will not apply to some children's families. It might be best to illustrate this by showing images of famous celebrities with their children. Good celebrities to use might include the royal family: Prince Philip, King Charles, Prince William and Prince George all look very similar.

Selective breeding

Through selective breeding, humans are able to make changes in animals and plants, making choices about which features they wish to develop and which they want to lose. In this way, farmers have selectively bred different varieties of cattle for better milk or meat production, or sheep for wool or meat. All the different types of brassica, such as broccoli, Savoy cabbage, kohl rabi and kale, were bred by humans from a single species of wild cabbage. The process of selective breeding is similar in principle to natural selection, but happens much faster as it relies less on chance pairings of organisms.

Sustainability link

Food security: look at how pest- or drought-resistant crops are being developed through selective breeding.

Dog breeders have, over thousands of years of selective breeding produced all the varieties of dog, choosing different features like size, body shape and coat colour. Cross-breeding between types of dog has produced dogs like the cockapoo, which has the friendly nature of a cocker spaniel and the hypoallergenic coat of a poodle.

It took 30,000 years to turn a wolf into a chihuahua. Well done humanity for that one!

Evolution and natural selection

Within a population, there is variation. All living things have slight differences to the others, based on the features they have inherited from their parents. Even siblings will be different. These differences can give some the edge over others.

The phrase '**survival of the fittest'** causes a lot of confusion. It doesn't mean that only the strongest survive. By 'fittest', we mean the best suited to the environment. These will have a better chance of survival, and so will reach adulthood and be able to breed, passing their useful features on to the next generation.

Evolution by natural selection relies on a few basic principles:

1. There is variation among individuals in a population. They are all slightly different.
2. This variation is passed from parents to their offspring.
3. There is competition for vital resources. Not every individual will survive to breed.
4. Those individuals best suited to their environment are more likely to survive and breed, passing their successful genes on to the next generation.

This can explain how a brown bear evolved into a polar bear. As they moved north, bears that had more body fat, or bigger paws, or paler fur would survive better in the cold, snowy conditions. This would give them an advantage over other bears, and they would survive to pass these characteristics on to the next generation. Over tens of thousands of years, the polar bear evolved as we know it today.

Darwin and Wallace

The two obvious scientists to study as part of this unit are Charles Darwin and Alfred Wallace. Charles Darwin developed his theory of evolution in the late 1830s, following his observations of the natural world while travelling on the HMS *Beagle*. At the same time, another English scientist called Alfred Russel Wallace had also been developing his theory of natural selection while travelling around Malaysia collecting animal specimens. In 1858, he wrote to Darwin outlining his ideas. This spurred Darwin into action and they published a joint paper outlining the theory of evolution by natural selection. Darwin's famous book *On the Origin of Species* was published in 1859 and immediately became a best-seller.

Darwin's finches

During his time on the Galapagos Islands, Darwin collected specimens of the different species of finch living on the island. By noticing that finches on the different islands had beaks that were adapted to their environment and realising that finches whose beaks weren't adapted wouldn't survive, Darwin was able to start working out his theory of evolution. The Galapagos finches are a classic example of adaptive radiation. Their common ancestor arrived on the islands a few million years ago. Since then, a single species has evolved into separate species that are adapted to fill different lifestyles.

Evidence for evolution

The evidence for evolution rests on five key points:

- Living things have adapted to best live in their environment.
- Life has existed on Earth for a very long time. There has been plenty of time for changes to happen.
- Fossils show us what life used to look like. Through fossils we can see changes in life forms over time.
- Characteristics are passed down from parents to offspring.
- Subtle changes might lead to a better chance of survival. These characteristics are passed down to the next generation.

As you teach this unit, keep referring to these five points.

Camouflage

Many animals have adapted different forms of camouflage to hide from predators. Some just match the colours of the environment around them, while others have adapted to look like sticks, twigs or even leaves.

An interesting example to look at is the peppered moth. The majority of moths were light coloured, with only a tiny proportion having the gene that made them dark coloured. Pollution from the Industrial Revolution coated the trees in soot. The light-peppered moth was no longer able to camouflage itself on the tree trunks, and so became easy to spot by birds. There was now an advantage to being a dark moth, as they were harder to spot, and they passed this gene on to their offspring. Within 100 years, 98 per cent of all peppered moths were dark. The change from pre-dominantly light to dark forms in industrial areas is known as 'industrial melanism'.

Challenges and misconceptions the children may have

Evolution is a subject area that has many misconceptions. Evolution is an incredibly slow process that takes place over thousands or millions of years. It is not something that can be easily observed in the classroom. Pupils might believe that animals and plants have always looked the same and have never changed.

A harder misconception to tackle is that animals 'want' to change to achieve a goal. It is hard to avoid saying that an organism is 'designed' for living in a particular environment, whereas in reality the organism has slowly adapted over many generations. Try to use the word 'adapted' instead of 'designed' whenever you talk about how organisms are suited to their habitat.

Children might have seen films where dinosaurs and humans lived side by side. It is important to look at the timeline of life on Earth and point out that dinosaurs were wiped out roughly 60 million years before the very first humans started to evolve.

If humans evolved from monkeys, why are there still monkeys?

A common misconception arises from the assumption that we have evolved from the chimpanzees and apes that you can see today. This is not true. We didn't evolve from chimps, but we share a common, monkey-like, ancestor that both humans and chimps evolved from. Explain to children that apes and chimps are our relatives, in the same way that they are related to their cousins or second cousins.

Making the learning real: Linking the unit to everyday life

Many children will have an interest in dinosaurs, which would provide a route into a discussion about how long ago they lived and why there were no humans around at the time. Children may have found fossils while out exploring, or maybe they have bought fossils from a shop. You can use these to start a discussion about fossils and what they can tell us.

Some children in your class may be part of a set of twins. This could be used to discuss what it is that makes us look the way we do, and why usually brothers and sisters look different.

Practical lesson ideas

Mixed-up animals

The children could cut up pictures or use computer software to build up new animals from the body parts of several different ones. They could then explain how these animals have adapted to a particular habitat, how they move, how they hunt or avoid predators, etc.

Camouflaged worms

Dye short lengths of cooked spaghetti different colours – red, blue, green. You could also use lengths of pipe cleaner or string. Toss them onto a marked-out area of grass and give the children 1 minute to collect them up. Which colours did they collect the most/least?

Bird beaks

Fill a bowl with raisins or seeds. Ask the children to use chopsticks and see how many seeds/raisins they can pick up and transfer to the empty bowl in 30 seconds. Do this several times to get an average. Then ask them to repeat this using tweezers. Discuss which tool was best for picking up the raisins? If they were a bird that mainly ate raisins, would they be better with a long beak like chopsticks or a small beak like tweezers?

Design a plant

The children could be asked to design and draw a plant that could live in a particular habitat such as a rainforest canopy, a pond or the desert. The children should consider the problems a plant might have living there and come up with ingenious ways to get around them. They could label these features and write about them. The children could even build a 3-D model of their plant from different materials.

Visualising deep time

An idea put forward by Horlock et al. (2015) is to use rice to visualise deep time. Use 1 grain of rice to represent one year. A 1kg packet of rice should hold around 50,000 grains of rice. A total of 20 bags of rice would represent 1 million years. A 1m³ box would be about 50 million. You would need 72 of these boxes to represent the 3.6 billion years of life on earth. You would need to fill a 6m x 6m classroom to a depth of 2m to represent deep time.

Cross-curricular links and opportunities

There are many cross-curricular links with art and design as well as literacy and numeracy, so be sure to talk to the coordinators in your school for help and advice.

Literacy There are opportunities here for role-play or debates. The children could carry out research into Charles Darwin and Alfred Wallace, and produce a presentation about their life. They could produce a short play or an animation to explain evolution.

The books *Moth* by Isabel Thomas (2018) and *The Molliebird* by Jules Pottle (2019) are great ways to combine storytelling with the science of evolution.

Numeracy There are opportunities for data collection and analysis by looking at class variation. The children could collect data on hair colour, eye colour, hand span, etc. They could link variables – for example, they could see if height is linked to reach. Data could be presented as different kinds of graph. They could also use a spreadsheet or a database to collect and present their data.

Religious education The children could find out about other creation myths – the different stories that cultures over the years have used to explain the earth and living things. They could read Native American, Maori or Maasai creation stories and compare them to the story of creation given in the Book of Genesis.

Geography and history Darwin's five-year voyage on HMS *Beagle* would provide a good link with geography. Children could plot his voyage on a map and find out about the different countries he visited. They could study Darwin and Wallace as part of a wider project about Victorian Britain.

Progression

This unit only appears in Year 6 but draws on a lot of knowledge covered earlier in school, from the features that different animals and plants have to classification of living things. Fossils were introduced in Year 3 and are further explored here, with reference to what the fossil records tell us about how living things have changed over time.

Suggested scientists

There are a great many naturalists and paleontologists who could be featured here that children might like to research. Some examples include:

- **Mary Anning** A nineteenth-century English palaeontologist whose discoveries along the Jurassic coast of Dorset contributed significantly to our understanding of prehistoric life.
- **Alice Roberts** British anatomist, biological anthropologist, author and television presenter known for her contributions to the fields of anthropology and archaeology.
- **Jean-Baptiste Lamarck** An eighteenth-century French naturalist and biologist, known for his early work on the theory of the inheritance of acquired characteristics.
- **Mary Leakey** A prominent British paleoanthropologist who made remarkable discoveries of hominid fossils in East Africa, including the famous fossil footprints at Laetoli.

Further reading and resources

App State: Deep Time Toolbox for Educators: https://earth.appstate.edu/outreach/deep-time-toolbox-educators
ASE: Mary Anning: www.ase.org.uk/mary-anning-fossil-hunters-story
BBC Teach: The Life and Work of Mary Anning: www.bbc.co.uk/programmes/p015gn89
Charles Darwin Trust: www.charlesdarwintrust.org/
Evolution for Primary Kids: https://evolutionforprimarykids.co.uk/
Evolution is Not Just a Theory: www.notjustatheory.com/

Natural History Museum: Spot the Adaptations in Darwin's Finches: www.nhm. ac.uk/schools/teaching-resources/galapagos-finches-show-beak-differences.html

OneZoom Tree of Life Explorer: www.onezoom.org/

Peppered Moth Game: https://askabiologist.asu.edu/peppered-moths-game/play. html

Primary Evolution: http://web.primaryevolution.com/

Thomas, I. (2019) *Moth: An Evolution Story*: https://isabelthomas.co.uk/project/ moth/

CHAPTER 8

Materials and Their Properties

Introduction

Materials are a fundamental part of our life. Everything around us, including ourselves, is made of different types of material – from the clothes we wear, the houses we live in, even the air we breathe and the water we drink.

Pupils can be confused about the meaning of the word **material**. They might only have heard the word in the context of clothes and fabrics. A material is anything made from **matter**, anything that is made from 'stuff' that physically occupies space and has mass.

Science knowledge you need before you can teach this topic

Comparing and grouping materials

The appearance and properties of materials may be used to group or classify them and determine their appropriateness for a specific function.

For many pupils, these classifications will be based on direct sensory experiences, how they feel and how they look. Allow them time to explore and sort a range of materials based on their own rules and then suggest others they could use.

We can group materials according to various properties:

- Texture: Is it rough or smooth, hard or soft?
- Flexibility: Can it bend or is it stiff?

- Waterproof: Does it allow water to pass through it? Is it porous?
- Transparency: Is the material transparent, translucent or opaque?
- Magnetic: Is the material magnetic or not?
- Conductivity: Does it conduct or insulate heat and electricity? Does it feel cold when you touch it?

Object vs. material

At KS1, pupils should be able to distinguish between an object and the material from which it is made. For example, pupils could investigate different types of ball made from different materials such as a tennis ball, ping-pong ball, squash ball and golf ball. How are they the same? How are they different? Which ball is the bounciest?

Teaching materials in the early years

In the early years, allow the pupils to explore the materials for themselves. The sand tray and water tray provide lots of opportunities for structured and unstructured exploration of different materials. You don't need anything fancy – at a pinch, a plastic storage crate will do the trick. Many accessories such as funnels, sponges and sieves can be picked up cheaply.

Linking properties to their uses

Different materials behave in different ways, and it is these different properties that make them suitable for particular uses. When designing new structures, engineers will select materials that are best suited to the job – based on their strength, flexibility, density and many other properties.

This can sometimes be hard for the pupils to understand. They may start with cyclical ideas about the use of materials for different jobs – for example, wellington boots are made from rubber.

The pupils should be able to identify the most important properties of any material used to create a particular object. For example, the function of an umbrella is to protect people from rain, therefore it must be made from a waterproof material that is also lightweight (so it can be carried), flexible (so it can be folded) and strong (so it can withstand heavy rain and wind).

Types of rocks and the rock cycle

Rocks are vitally important to the world we live in. We use them in the construction of buildings, walls and roads, for sculpture and decoration. They are even ground up and used in products such as toothpaste and makeup.

The KS2 unit about rocks starts by looking at different types of rock and how they can be grouped by their simple properties. It then explores why we use different rocks for different purposes. Start by taking the pupils on a walk around the school site to see how different rocks are being used.

What is a rock?

Rock is a natural material, such as slate, marble or limestone. Not all natural hard materials are rocks. Building materials such as brick and concrete can look a lot like rock but are not strictly rocks.

Properties of rocks

Rocks can be investigated using different properties, such as hardness, permeability, porosity and the effect of acid. You can buy rock kits to do this with from most educational suppliers.

- **Hardness** Rub different rocks against one another to see if they make a mark. This is something called the Mohs scale, which ranks rocks in order of how hard or soft they are.
- **Permeability** Drip water onto the rocks using a pipette. Does the water get soaked up by the rock or does it sit on the surface?
- **Porosity** Weigh the rocks dry, then immerse them in water for 5 minutes. Do they bubble? Remove the rocks, pat them dry and weigh them again. Which rocks have soaked up the most water?
- **The effect of acid** Using a pipette and some strong vinegar, drip them onto the rock samples. Rocks that contain calcium carbonate, such as chalk, marble and limestone will fizz.

Visit the Royal Society of Chemistry website for a guide on how to carry out these tests.

Types of rock

There are three broad categories of rock, depending on how the rock has been formed.

- **Igneous rock** Formed when molten lava or magma from inside the Earth cools and solidifies. This can happen when lava leaves a volcano in an eruption, but it can also happen below the surface, when magma gets close to the crust and cools. Igneous rocks often have crystals in them, formed as they cool. Igneous rocks include granite and basalt.
- **Sedimentary rock** When rocks are eroded by wind and rain, they form a powder or sediment. This sediment ends up in lakes and rivers where it sinks to the bottom and becomes compressed. Sedimentary rock forms as layers of sediment (strata) compress the layers beneath them. Sedimentary rocks often contain fossils, as living things die and end up being buried by sediment. Examples of sedimentary rock include sandstone, limestone and chalk.
- **Metamorphic rock** Produced when igneous or metamorphic rocks experience intense heat or pressure. Metamorphic rocks form deep in the Earth's crust as the pressure of rock layers above them increases, along with the temperature. Examples of metamorphic rock include soapstone, marble and slate.

Sustainability link

Children can find out where different rocks come from and the environmental impact of quarrying.

Fossils

A fossil is the preserved remains or traces of a dead organism. Fossils tell us what animals and plants that lived millions of years ago looked like. We can tell a lot from fossils. Sometimes whole organisms fossilise, but you can learn a lot from smaller fossils such as teeth, leaves and even poo!

Soils

Soil is one of the world's most precious natural resources. It is vital for plant growth, providing food and materials for humans and animals; it regulates water by filtering out pollutants and can reduce flood risks; and it is home to a vast array of animals (OPAL, 2015).

When asked what soil is, children frequently suggest that its main role is for growing plants (SPACE, 1993). Children might think of soil as something dull and brown, but soils come in a range of different types and differ from place to place.

Soil itself is not a single substance but a combination of rocks, minerals, plant materials, animal materials, other microorganisms (which make organic matter), air and water. Plants then grow in these rock particles and when these (and animals) die, they decay and produce humus.

Decaying humus breaks down to release minerals for plants to utilise. Soils can have different properties, depending on the rocks that form them and the organic matter created. Soil contains different layers of material, including topsoil, subsoil, weathered rocks and bedrock.

Sustainability links

Children could look at making their own compost or setting up a wormery. They could find out about desertification, where human impact can damage the soil and make it very hard to sustain any plants.

States of matter and particle theory

Everything that we can see, smell or touch is made from tiny particles called atoms. These can be arranged in different ways to make the solids, liquids and gases that make up your body and the world around you.

Asking the pupils to categorise objects as solids, liquids and gases, and including ambiguous materials such as the objects below, can help draw out these kinds of misconception and allow for discussion.

When asked to draw a solid, pupils will often draw something large and heavy. Objects such as a bag of rice or salt can be confusing since they don't behave exactly how a solid should – they can change their shape (Varelas et al., 2007). Similarly, a straw is not thought to be a solid because it is hollow.

Solids, liquids and gases

As far as KS2 is concerned, there are three states of matter: solids, liquids and gases.

- **Solids** These are hard and generally difficult to compress. They have a fixed shape.
- **Liquids** Liquids can flow and take the shape of the bottom of their container. They can't be squashed.
- **Gases** Gases are light and have no fixed shape or volume. They expand to fill whatever container they are put in.

(In reality, it is believed that there are actually at least seven known states of matter, including plasma, but let's keep it simple!)

Many objects are composite materials – they contain more than one type of material. Think of a football or a balloon, the skin is a solid, but it has a gas inside it. Toothpaste is a **colloid** – a mixture of thick liquid with small pieces of solid inside it. A **foam**, such as shaving foam or a sponge, is a mixture of liquid with bubbles of gas throughout. Some liquids are **emulsions** (containing solid particles) – for example, blood, milk and paint.

The particle model

The particle model does not form part of the KS2 national curriculum and it is a difficult concept for some, but there's evidence that teaching it in KS2 does make explaining solids, liquids and gases in Year 4 easier (Skamp, 2005). This also helps when talking about sound and vibrations later in Year 4, when we need to talk about how vibrations travel in different materials.

Evidence suggests that primary teachers should place emphasis on the macroscopic properties of matter first (Skamp, 2005) and the teacher needs to decide whether going into the detail about particles is appropriate, in terms of content, context and the ability of the children (Lee and Tan, 2004).

A solid is made of particles that are held together strongly in a fixed regular pattern. A solid is rigid and has a definite volume and shape. A cup will stay cup-shaped wherever you put it. Because the particles are so close together, a solid cannot be compressed.

A liquid is a material made of particles that are very close together, but not as tightly bound as in a solid so they have more freedom to move. This means that a liquid has a definite volume but no fixed shape. It can flow and take the shape of its container, but because the particles are close together, a liquid cannot be compressed.

In gases, the particles are not joined together and so are free to move and spread out. A gas has no fixed shape or volume and will expand to fill the entire space available to it.

Changing state

Ice, water and water vapour all consist of exactly the same water molecules, but in different formations. There is no chemical difference between these substances, just that the particles have arranged themselves differently. If an ice cube melts into water, the total amount of particles will stay the same, so the mass of ice will be the same as the water.

Most substances we know of can exist as solid, liquid or gas. They may have very high or very low melting points, but eventually they can be changed. Iron can be turned into a liquid in a furnace. It is even possible to get solid oxygen or nitrogen if they are cooled enough. Oxygen freezes at –218°C and nitrogen at –210°C!

Melting and freezing

When heat energy is supplied to a solid, the particles vibrate more vigorously. Eventually, they can break free from each other and move freely, becoming a liquid. This change is called **melting**. Cooling a liquid down will cause the particles to move more slowly. If a liquid is cooled enough, its particles join back together to form a solid. This is called **freezing**. Children will often associate freezing with water turning into ice and cold temperatures, but the term applies to all liquids which become solids. Molten chocolate freezes to a solid at around 35°C, while molten iron freezes at around 1535°C.

Evaporating and condensing

Heating a liquid makes its particles move more quickly. With enough energy, some particles near the surface overcome the forces of attraction and escape to become a gas. This is called **evaporation**. If the temperature rises high enough, particles not just on the surface but anywhere in the liquid start to escape and form bubbles. At **boiling point**, the temperature remains the same, however strongly it is heated, until all the liquid has become a gas. This takes place at a specific temperature for each pure liquid. In pure water, this temperature is 100°C.

Cooling a gas down to below its boiling point will cause particles to move more slowly. The gas changes back to a liquid, which is called **condensing**.

The water cycle

Through the water cycle we can show that the Earth is a closed system. Water circulates in a constant cycle between the ocean, the atmosphere and the land. Water can be moved in many different forms, such as water vapour, rain, snow or hail.

The Sun's energy warms liquid water in seas and lakes, making it **evaporate** into water vapour and rise into the atmosphere. Water within plants is also lost to the atmosphere in a process called transpiration. As this vapour rises, the air cools and the water vapour **condenses** into tiny water droplets, forming clouds.

Clouds are made from tiny droplets of water light enough to be held up by air currents. The water droplets in clouds can eventually become so large that they fall as rain or snow (precipitation). The water can then form rivers and flow to a lake or sea where it starts the cycle again. Sometimes water can spend thousands of years locked up as snow or ice before melting and getting back to the sea.

This cycle has taken place for billions of years. Only a fraction of the water has been lost into space. So, in any glass of water there will be molecules of water that were drunk by dinosaurs, millions of years ago!

Sustainability links

Look at water usage and the need for fresh water. Children could investigate how much water is used through different activities such as showering or using a dishwasher. Most water utility companies will provide this information online. The children could research different ways of saving water and plan a campaign to save water at home or at school.

Physical changes

In a physical change, no new substance is made and it can be easily reversed. As well as changes of state, physical changes can also involve processes such as dissolving.

Dissolving

Dissolving is a simple physical change to explore in the classroom. The liquids that allow dissolving are known as **solvents** and the solid that dissolved is known as the **solute**.

When a substance such as sugar dissolves, the granules of sugar break into small particles that are dispersed throughout the liquid until they are too small to see. The mixture of water and sugar particles is called a **solution**.

The dissolved sugar has not been chemically changed; sugar particles have not reacted with water particles. It is still sugar, with the same properties as before. Dissolving is a physical change.

You could demonstrate a model for dissolving to the pupils using a tray or shallow box with a layer of rice covering the bottom to represent particles of water. Add a handful of dried peas to represent the particles of sugar. Shake it up and eventually all the peas are mixed in among the rice.

Where does it go?

Question: What happens if you dissolve 5g of sugar in 100g of water? How much does the solution weigh? 100g? 105g or something else?

When something like sugar is dissolved, it doesn't vanish – its particles have just become mixed up with the particles of water. You can prove they are still there by tasting the liquid. You can still taste the sugar.

If you add 5g of sugar to 100g of water, the overall weight of the solution is 105g. The sugar is still there. If you evaporate the water, the sugar is left behind.

Separating mixtures

A mixture forms when two or more materials are combined together but do not undergo a chemical change. Although the mixture may look different from its constituent parts, the original materials do not chemically change and no new material is made.

Physical or mechanical processes can usually separate mixtures, although this is sometimes not always possible. Processes to explore include filtering, sieving, evaporating and chromatography (chromatography is a way of separating a mixture of inks).

For examples of separating mixtures, the Royal Society of Chemistry website has some great resources.

Chemical changes

A chemical change is a process in which two or more substances react together to produce a new substance. The chemicals might join together in new ways or break apart and rejoin, forming new chemical substances. Chemical changes cannot be easily reversed. They are known as irreversible reactions. Examples of chemical reactions include cooking, burning and rusting.

Signs of a chemical reaction

There are often noticeable signs that a chemical reaction is taking place. There might be a flame or bubbles of gas produced. It might change colour or give off light (as in glowsticks).

The reaction might produce heat (exothermic) or absorb heat and get colder (endothermic).

Chemical changes in the classroom

A challenge in teaching this topic is finding good practical opportunities that are safe to do in the primary classroom and do not require complicated equipment. As with all practical work, refer to CLEAPPS and other safety guides, and always carry out a risk assessment. It's a good idea to test them out yourself before you use them with a class.

For more on health and safety, see Chapter 18.

Make clear the differences between chemical and physical changes.

- A chemical change is a reaction where new substances are produced. It is not easily reversible.
- A physical change is a reaction where no new substances are produced. They are usually reversible.

Sustainability links

The children could look at how paper, plastic and glass are made, and how they can be recycled.

Mixtures and compounds

Some children find it difficult to understand the difference between what we mean by a mixture and a compound. They have very specific meanings in science.

A mixture forms when two or more materials are combined together but do not undergo a chemical change. Although the mixture may be very different from its constituent parts, the original materials do not chemically change and no new material is made.

Physical or mechanical processes can usually separate mixtures, although this is not always possible – for example, when one substance forms a coating around another. Mixtures can take the form of solids, liquids or gases, or they can even be a combination of all three.

An element is the simplest form of a chemical substance, containing a single type of atom. Examples of elements include gold, copper, oxygen and hydrogen.

A compound is made from several elements that join together in a reaction. Water is a compound formed from the reaction between hydrogen gas and oxygen gas. One molecule of water is made from two hydrogen atoms joined to one oxygen (H_2O). Other compounds, such as plastics or the proteins in our bodies, can be made up of long chains of hundreds of atoms.

Many of the materials we encounter each day are compounds. Many compounds can be put into mixtures without reacting further. For example, salt and water are both compounds, but they can be mixed together to form salt water, which is a mixture.

Challenges and misconceptions the children may have

Common misconceptions the pupils have include the idea that since gases can't be seen, they don't exist and have no mass. They might also think that water freezing or melting causes a change in mass. You can actively assess understanding in these areas – for instance, by asking pupils to draw and annotate pictures and diagrams to demonstrate their understanding as they progress through the topic. Tytler et al. (2006) used a sequence of activities to model changes of state and relate to particle diagrams. Pupils observe different activities and were encouraged to use the idea of particles in the diagrams they drew to explain what was happening. Allow them to observe phenomena for themselves, then ask them to explain what they see.

Some children may be confused about the difference between burning and melting, and the production of steam and smoke. It is important that it is clear to the children that burning is a chemical reaction in which new products, including smoke, are produced. Children might believe that when something burns, parts of it vanish and no longer exist. They might have seen paper burn and only a small pile of ash remain. Burning is a chemical reaction with the main products being carbon dioxide and water vapour. Because these are both invisible gases, they can't be seen. Some of the carbon in the paper becomes smoke, while the rest falls as ash and it is this that we see when something burns.

Children might think that the particles inside the different states of matter are different – that the particles get bigger or smaller or change shape when moving from a solid to a liquid.

Making the learning real: linking the unit to everyday life

You could relate the discussion of materials to situations that the pupils will be familiar with. They will know that different clothes are suitable for different weather conditions. This could be linked this to the KS1 seasonal changes unit; they should know that some materials are better for keeping them warm on a cold day and that some coats are more waterproof than others. They could look at objects such as their lunchboxes or pencil cases and think about what they are made from and why.

There are many physical and chemical changes that take place in our everyday lives that children should be familiar with, which can provide a starting point for discussion. They will have seen things burning, such as candles or charcoal on a barbeque. They will have seen many examples of cooking such as frying eggs. They will have experienced other common chemical reactions such as fireworks, sparklers or glowsticks.

Practical lesson ideas

Materials/rocks walk

Take the children on a walk around the school and look for examples of different materials. Discuss why each material was used for that particular job. Use a digital camera to record examples.

Silly materials

Play a game of 'Silly Materials'. Ask the children to think of different items, then list a silly material to make it from. They can then think about the actual material and why it is used.

You could use Michael Rosen's poem 'Woolly Saucepan' as a way to introduce this, or videos of an actual chocolate teapot being made (search Google for 'chocolate teapot video' – there are loads!).

Three little pigs

The story of 'The Three Little Pigs' can be a fun way of introducing the idea of the benefits of different building materials. Give the pupils a range of materials and ask them to build a house for the pigs. Give each group time to plan and build a house, then use a hairdryer as the big bad wolf to see if each house can withstand a huff and a puff.

Make plastic from milk and vinegar

Pour about half a pint of warm whole milk into a bowl, then add a tablespoon of white vinegar and stir. Once the milk has curdled, strain it and keep the solid material that has formed. Place this on a paper towel to dry it out. It can then be moulded and left to dry hard, and finally it can be painted and varnished.

Cross-curricular links and opportunities

In literacy, there are opportunities to link to stories such as 'The Three Little Pigs'. The children could brainstorm descriptions of different materials and use these to write simple poems. They could use properties of materials to look at opposites, such as flexible and inflexible, or transparent and opaque.

In geography, the children could look at houses around the world, and the materials used to build them. This could include igloos made from ice and houses made from mud and straw.

In history, the children could look at different historical buildings, such as the pyramids or Roman temples, and what materials were used to build them.

Chemical changes could be linked to design and technology by investigating chemical changes in the context of cooking. The children can make cakes, fudge or popcorn. They could make different types of bread and look at the difference between leavened and unleavened bread and what makes it rise.

Progression

The study of materials progresses from a look at different materials and their properties and considering how those properties are linked to their use. Rocks and their properties and uses are also considered. The three states of matter are then introduced and the idea of physical changes. Properties of materials are investigated in more detail and finally chemical changes are explored and compared to physical changes.

Suggested scientists

There are a great many materials scientists who could be featured here that children might like to research. Some examples include:

- **Stephanie Kwolek** Inventor of Kevlar, used in bullet-proof vests.
- **Ruth Benerito** Inventor of non-iron, wash-and-wear fabric.
- **Mary Anderson** Inventor of the windscreen wiper.

Further reading and resources

Curious Minds (2015) 'Have you drunk dinosaur pee?': https://youtu.be/KK64DqplyOs
Earth Science Education Unit: www.earthscienceeducation.com/resources/index.htm
Nicholson, D. (2022) 'Why you should teach about particles in Year 4': www.sciencefix.co.uk/2022/04/why-you-should-teach-about-particles-in-year-4
Royal Society of Chemistry: Rocks and Soils: https://edu.rsc.org/primary-science/rocks-and-soils-thats-chemistry/1795.article

CHAPTER 9

Forces and Magnets

Introduction

Forces are invisible, but they are a vital part of our lives. Without an understanding of forces, our houses would collapse and aeroplanes would never leave the ground.

The invention of levers, wheels, gears and pulleys transformed the way we once lived. It allowed our ancestors to build bigger and more complex places in which to live and work, allowed them to irrigate fields, grind flour, transport heavy loads, travel to distant places, and much more.

Science knowledge you need before you can teach this topic

Pushes and pulls

Forces can be described as a push or a pull, or a twist (push one side, pull the other). In Early Years, pupils experience a range of toys, craft activities and play equipment that involve pushing or pulling. The children could go on a push-and-pull walk to see examples of things being pushed and pulled.

At Key Stage 1, pupils are reintroduced to the idea of pushes and pulls within the Year 2 Uses of Everyday Materials unit in the context of the changing shape of a material such as modelling clay. As the children play with the modelling clay, ask them what words can they use to describe what they do to the clay (squeeze, twist, bend, squash, flatten, etc).

May the Force be with you

It might help by thinking of all the different, non-science uses of the word 'force' that we use. 'May the Force be with you' is one example, but also words and phrases like 'Armed Forces', 'Police Force', 'A force of nature', etc.

For most of us, the word 'force' often implies getting something done or making something do something. You can then introduce what scientists mean by the word 'force', which is a push or a pull.

A force can cause an object to start moving, stop moving, speed up, slow down or change shape.

Forces are measured in **Newtons** (N) and can be measured using a force meter/Newton meter.

Magnets

Magnetic forces can act at a distance, without direct contact, like gravity. Stick a magnet on top of a small toy car and push it with another magnet – it's possible to make the car move without having to touch it.

In Early Years and KS1, pupils explore using magnets. See what objects stick to a magnet and which ones don't. The children could sort materials into two groups based on whether they are magnetic or not.

Young pupils do not generally know about what materials a magnet will stick to, often including metals such as gold and aluminium, but also non-metals such as wood, cloth and glass (Christidou et al., 2009). Pupils might have seen cartoons and movies where a super magnet attracts every single metal object nearby, which doesn't help with this misconception.

Magnetic materials are always made of metal, but not all metals are magnetic. Iron, nickel and cobalt are magnetic. Steel is magnetic because it contains iron (but some types of stainless steel are not magnetic.)

Magnets have two poles, called **North** and **South**. If you hold two magnets close together with opposite poles pointing towards each other, they will attract and stick together. If you hold the magnets with the same poles together, North against North or South against South, then the magnets will push each other away or repel.

A magnetic compass works because planet Earth has its own magnetic field. It acts as if there is a giant bar magnet inside it. What we call the North Pole of a magnet is technically the north-seeking pole. If you hang a magnet on a piece of string and allow it to move freely, the N pole points towards to the North Pole of the Earth.

Making a magnet

It is possible to turn a steel paperclip into a magnet. First straighten it out and then use a regular magnet and stroke the paperclip repeatedly in one direction only. After ten strokes, see if it will pick up another paperclip. If not, stroke it another ten times and repeat.

This works because the atoms inside a piece of metal act like tiny mini-magnets called 'domains'. Usually, they are all pulling in different directions and cancelling out each other's effects, so the material is not magnetic.

If you stroke a metal such as iron, steel or cobalt with another magnet, the domains can all line up and point in the same direction. This reinforces their overall effect and the metal becomes magnetic. In non-magnetic metals, the domains cannot move, so the metal cannot become magnetic.

Over time, they will move back out of line and lose their magnetism again. This is also why dropping and mistreating school magnets eventually makes them become weaker and lose their magnetism, so treat them nicely!

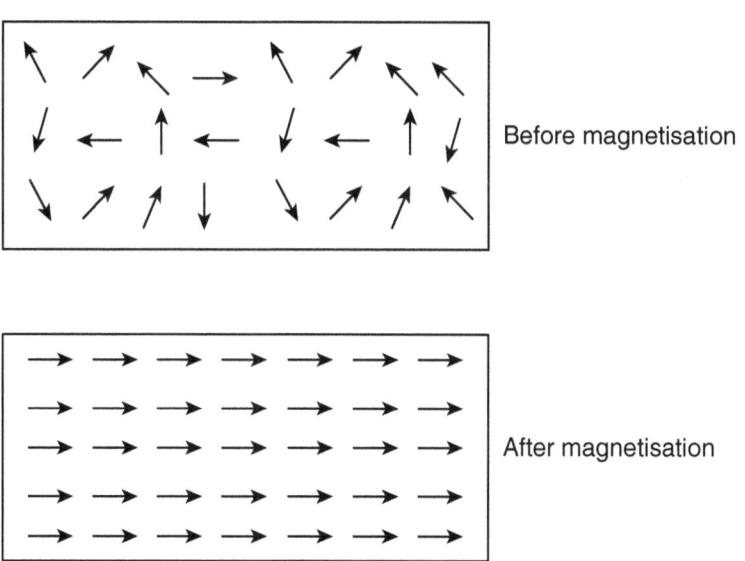

Before magnetisation

After magnetisation

Figure 9.1   Domains in a magnetic material before and after magnetisation

Static objects and balanced forces

If an object is stationary, then all the forces on it must be balanced. So, if a book sitting on a table is pushing down with a force of 5N, then the table is also pushing upwards on the book with an identical force of 5N. This is called a **reactive force**.

If these forces were not balanced, then the book would either fall through the table or be pushed up into the air.

Moving objects

Forces can make an object speed up, slow down, change shape and change direction. On Earth, for something to keep moving, such as a car or a plane, a force needs to be applied, otherwise air resistance and friction will slow it down and bring it to a stop. When something like a car is travelling at a steady speed, all the forces acting upon it are balanced.

Balanced forces

A common misconception is that forces always act in pairs that are equal and opposite. The misconception comes from Newton's third law of motion: 'For every action there is an equal and opposite reaction.' But if this was true, then nothing would ever move because the forces would always be perfectly balanced.

While it is true that forces do usually act in pairs, it does not automatically mean they are equal. Forces are only balanced if the object is moving at a steady speed or not moving at all.

When a car starts moving, the force pushing it forward is greater than the friction/ air resistance trying to slow it down, so it starts to accelerate. When it is travelling at a steady speed along the road, the forward force is equal to the air resistance/ friction. These forces are now balanced.

If the driver applies the brakes, the forces are unbalanced again; the resistance/ friction is now higher than the force moving the car forwards, so the car slows down and will eventually stop.

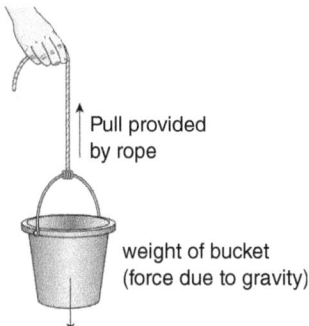

Pull provided
by rope

weight of bucket
(force due to gravity)

Figure 9.2   Forces acting on an object

Why do things fall?

The force that pulls things to the centre of the Earth (and all other planets) is called gravity. The larger and heavier the object, the greater the pull of gravity. An object as massive as the Sun has a strong enough pull of gravity to keep all the planets in the solar system in orbit around it, even as far out as Pluto and beyond.

Gravity is different on other planets because their mass is different. Some planets like Jupiter have a much higher pull of gravity than Earth. Some planets like Mercury have a much lower pull of gravity.

Mass and weight

In everyday language, we use the words 'mass' and 'weight' to mean the same thing, but for a scientist they mean slightly different things.

Your mass is how much of you there is, and your weight is the force you exert on the floor because of gravity.

- **Mass** is the amount of material or 'matter' in an object measured in kilograms (kg). The mass of an astronaut would be the same on Earth as it would be in space because he or she hasn't gained or lost any mass going into space.
- **Weight** is a force that changes in relation to the force of gravity. On Earth, gravity causes objects to accelerate towards its centre with a force of approximately

10N for every kilogram. An astronaut with a mass of 60kg has a weight of 600N on Earth. On the Moon, the pull of gravity is much less – about one sixth of that on Earth. A 60kg astronaut would only weigh 100N on the moon.

Air resistance and friction

If you throw a ball on Earth, the ball will eventually come to a stop because of forces such as friction, gravity and air resistance. These forces act on any moving object and eventually bring it to a stop. But if an astronaut in space was to throw a ball, then it would keep moving forever. The ball would keep going in a straight line and it would only stop (or change direction) if it hit another object or was pulled by the gravity of something very big such as a star or a planet. This would apply another force to the ball, which would change how it moved.

Newton's first law of motion states that an object will continue at a constant speed and in the same direction unless a force acts upon it. This means that even if an object is travelling at high speed, no force is required to maintain the speed. A force is only required if the object is to change the speed at which it is moving. Hence, a force is required for acceleration, deceleration or a change of direction.

A good demonstration of air resistance is to make parachutes out of thin paper or plastic sheet. Use a toy doll or blob of modelling clay to provide the weight and attach it with string to the corners of the parachute. Compare the time to fall with and without the parachute. The air resistance on the parachute will slow down the fall. Experiment with different sizes and shapes of parachute or different materials.

Friction

Friction is the force created between two surfaces when they rub together. Rough surfaces create more friction than smooth surfaces.

Friction can be useful. We need a high grip between the soles of our shoes and the ground, or between our car tyres and the road. Brakes rely on friction to slow down a car or bike.

Other times, friction can be something we want to reduce; we will add oil or lubricant to door hinges, the hubs of our bicycles to reduce friction and make them move more easily.

You can introduce friction as something that produces heat and allow pupils to feel the frictional forces by rubbing their hands together.

Air resistance

Air resistance is the force that acts between a moving object and the air molecules around it, slowing down the object.

To see the effect of air resistance, drop a sheet of paper and watch how it falls, then crumple it into a ball and drop it again. The mass of the paper hasn't changed, but the ball of paper falls much faster because it is in contact with less air as it falls, so it experiences less air resistance. Mass has no effect on how fast something falls (see below).

Modern cars and planes are designed to be streamlined, to reduce air resistance and move faster.

A parachute increases the air resistance and slows down the parachutist so that they can land safely.

Simple machines: levers, pulleys and gears

The three simple machines outlined by the national curriculum are levers, pulleys and gears. Let's look at each of these.

Levers

Levers can be demonstrated by using a meter rule or metal rod to lift a heavy object. A simple demonstration is to show how to push open a door. If you push close to the hinge, it is very hard to move the door; if you push near where the handle is, it should be very easy. The door is acting as a lever. You have to move a lot more, but you can use a much lower force.

Pulleys

Like a lever, pulleys trade force for distance. Using several pulleys, you would need to pull a rope over a longer distance but with a much lower force, allowing you to lift a heavy object easily.

Pulleys can be bought from educational suppliers or can be built from cotton reels and wooden skewers.

Gears

Gears are wheels with teeth that interlock together. Turning one gear makes the other one turn. If the gears are different sizes, they can be used to increase the power of a turning force. Turning a small wheel slowly will move the larger wheel slower but with more force.

You can explore gears with simple toys with interlocking gears. You could even bring in a bicycle to look at how its gears work.

Exploring forces

There are many different STEM challenges that the pupils can take part in to explore forces with real-world applications and problem-solving opportunities. Challenge the pupils to build the tallest tower out of spaghetti or protect an egg from falling.

Challenges and misconceptions the children may have

There is a common misconception that forces always act in pairs that are equal and opposite. If this was true, then nothing would ever move. The misconception comes from a misunderstanding of Newton's third law of motion: 'For every action there is an equal and opposite reaction', meaning that if you are pushing against the ground, the ground is pushing back against you. Children may have heard this being said and think that every force must automatically have an equal and opposite partner.

Another misconception is that heavy objects will fall faster than lighter objects. This is not true. The mass of an object has no effect on how fast it falls. Both objects will be pulled down with the same force of gravity, but air resistance will have an effect, so some objects may be slowed because of air resistance. If you remove the air, there is no air resistance. A bowling ball and a feather will fall at exactly the same rate. There is an excellent video from the Brian Cox series *Human Universe* which demonstrates this. Apollo 15 astronaut David Scott also proved it by dropping a hammer and a feather on the Moon.

Making the learning real: linking the unit to everyday life

Relate this topic to real-world examples that the children would have experienced. They may not know the word 'friction', but they will know about 'grip'. They should be aware of situations when good grip is useful, such as between their shoes and the ground or under the wheels of their bicycle. They have probably experienced icy pavements or wet floors where friction is low and they slide about. They will probably know that you need to put oil on objects to help them move better. In scientific language, this reduces the friction between the moving surfaces.

There are many real-world examples of machines using levers, pulleys and gears that the children might already know about, such as cranes or bicycles. You can explore the workings on these simple machines in the classroom by looking a bicycle gears, building simple pulley rigs with one or two pulleys or trying to lift objects with levers.

Practical lesson ideas

Build bridges

Challenge the children to build the strongest bridge from a single sheet of A4 paper. Just by folding it in different ways, can they make one that can support the most weight over a 15cm gap? Hint: triangles are very strong shapes. Websites such as The Rochester Bridge Trust have some good guides to building and testing different types of bridge.

Balloon-powered rocket cars

The children can build simple cars from foam and cardboard, with cardboard discs for wheels and straws, and barbeque skewers acting as axles. Power each car with the same size balloon, pointing backwards to push it along. Challenge the children to build a car that will travel the furthest or the fastest.

Explore coins

Get a selection of 1p and 2p coins and use a magnet to see if the coins are magnetic are not. Look at the dates to find the pattern. You should find that copper coins made before 1992 were mainly copper and are not magnetic. After 1992, they were mainly made of steel and are magnetic. The same thing happened with 5p and 10p coins in 2011.

Paper helicopters

Make a paper spinner out of a piece of paper and explore the factors that affect how long it takes to fall to the ground. Change the length of the wings, the size of the spinner and the type of paper the spinner is made from.

Cross-curricular links and opportunities

This topic provides great opportunities for projects that incorporate design and technology skills.

Children can design, build and test cars, rockets or bridges, for example, and investigate the forces acting on them. Small-scale models can be linked to real-world examples, such as how to make cars more aerodynamic. The children can use computing skills to record and present their findings. Data loggers with light gates can be used for timing and measuring the speed of moving objects.

Children could look at the cartoons of Heath Robinson or Rube Goldberg and design their own amazing contraptions to solve everyday problems. They could research some of the inventions of the artist Leonardo da Vinci such as his glider or submarine.

The many different investigations available provide plenty of maths opportunities, such as data handling and graph-drawing. Gears can be used to teach about ratios.

Links could be made between forces and physical education, looking at the different forces involved in track and field events. They could look at the use of levers, pulleys and gears in gym equipment.

The topic of forces also provides some great links with history topics, especially when looking at the types of machine available at the time. The children could find out how the Egyptians used simple levers and wheels to build the pyramids or how an Archimedes' screw could pump water to irrigate crops. They could look at how medieval trebuchets and catapults worked and build their own model versions. They could find out about some of the important machines of the Industrial Revolution, such as the steam engine.

Progression

Children start by looking at forces in terms of pushes and pulls. They then look at magnets as an example of a force, linking to materials. They look at moving objects and begin to think about friction. Later, they look at gravity as a pulling force and link it to the Earth and Space unit. Friction is explored again, along with air and water resistance. They then explore simple machines.

Suggested scientists

A great many physicists and engineers could be featured here who children might like to research. Some examples include:

- **The Wright brothers** Inventors of the airplane. Achieved the first powered, controlled and sustained flight in 1903, which revolutionised human transportation.
- **Isaac Newton** Known for his theory of gravity and the laws of motion. Laid the foundations for modern physics and mathematics with his groundbreaking work in the seventeenth century.
- **Galileo Galilei** Italian scientist. Made pioneering contributions to our understanding of gravity and acceleration through his experiments and astronomical observations.

Further reading and resources

Build a basic paper helicopter spinner: www.wikihow.com/Create-a-Paper-Helicopter

Brian Cox visits the world's biggest vacuum: https://youtu.be/E43-CfukEgs

Forces and Motion Simulator: https://phet.colorado.edu/en/simulations/forces-and-motion-basics

The Rochester Bridge Trust: 'Learning about bridges': https://rochesterbridgetrust.org.uk/learning-activities/learning-about-bridges/

STEM Learning: 'Paper helicopters': www.stem.org.uk/resources/elibrary/resource/34163/paper-helicopters-science

CHAPTER 10

The Earth in Space

Introduction

Humans have been fascinated with space for thousands of years. Early civilisations, such as the Ancient Egyptians, Chinese, Mayans and Babylonians, studied the stars and the Moon. Our Sun is just one of millions of stars that make up a galaxy called the Milky Way and that is just one of billions of galaxies that make up the known Universe. It's hard not to be a little overwhelmed once you start talking about space. To quote Douglas Adams: 'Space is big. Really big. You just won't believe how vastly, hugely, mindbogglingly big it is.'

Space as a topic doesn't appear in the national curriculum until Year 5, but there's no reason it can't appear in other years as part of other topic areas, perhaps looking at constellations when studying Ancient Greece, or the role of Stonehenge in tracking the Sun when looking at the Stone Age or Bronze Age.

With NASA aiming to put humans back on the Moon by the end of 2025, with Mars the goal after that in the 2030s, we could be living in some very exciting times for space exploration. Who knows, one of the first humans to set foot on Mars could be sitting in your classroom right now!

Safety warning

When carrying out any activity using the Sun, children should be warned that it is not safe to look directly at the Sun, even when wearing dark glasses.

Science knowledge you need before you can teach this topic

Days, months and years

The Earth is one of eight planets that travels around the Sun in what is called a solar system. This **heliocentric** model (the Sun at the centre) was first proposed by Copernicus in 1543. Before then, it was thought that the Earth was at the centre of the universe and everything revolved around it. This is the **geocentric** model.

The time for a planet to make one spin on its axis is known as a **day**. It takes the Earth 365 and a quarter days to make one complete orbit of the Sun. We call this a **year**. We add up the extra quarter days and every four years add a whole day to the calendar (this is a leap year).

A **moon** is an object that orbits a planet. Our planet has just one moon, but other planets have many more. Our Moon orbits the Earth once every 27 days. We call this a **month** (or moonth!). The Moon actually orbits the Earth 13 times in a year, but for various reasons, ancient civilisations preferred to base a calendar around 12 months instead. This is a long story worth looking at in history!

How do we get day and night?

At dawn, the Sun appears to rise in the East, becoming high in the sky by the middle of the day; at dusk, it sets in the West. In reality, it is not the Sun that is moving but the Earth

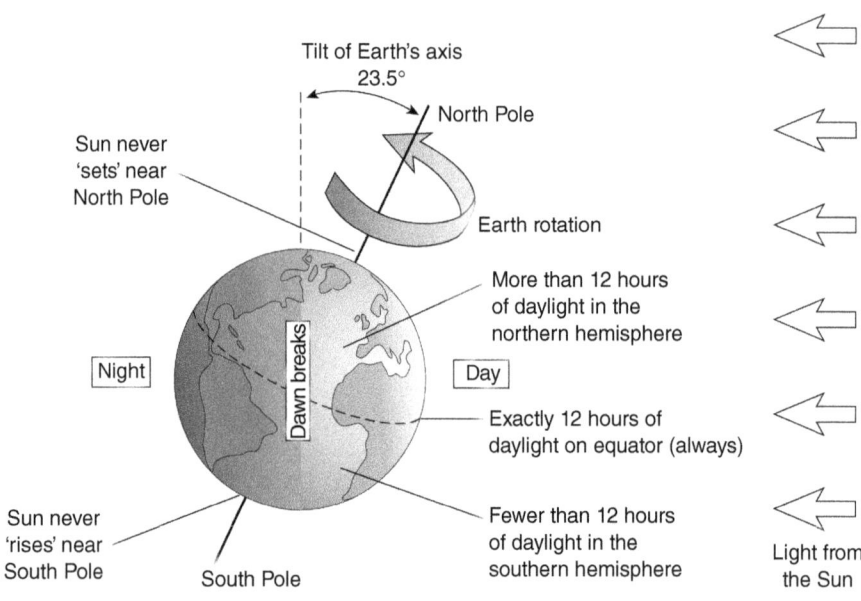

Figure 10.1   Day and night (June)

as it orbits around the Sun. Over the course of a day, the Earth rotates, anticlockwise around an invisible line called the axis. The axis runs from the North Pole to the South Pole.

Night and day

At any time, half the Earth is facing the Sun and is lit up by sunlight. We call this day. At the same time, half the Earth is facing away from the Sun, receiving no sunlight at all. We call this night.

Motion of the Earth, Sun and Moon

The Earth moves around the Sun in an elliptical orbit. It is held in place by the gravitational pull of the Sun. At the same time, the Moon is moving around the Earth, also in an elliptical orbit.

How do the seasons change?

In KS1, pupils should understand that there are different seasons, but they do not need to explain why.

The KS1 Seasonal Changes unit is best set up in September and run as an ongoing project through the course of the year. Weather monitoring and observing plants can then be run once a week or once a month to build up a bank of observations. This data can then be presented and discussed towards the end of the school year. Do remember to save any images and weather data centrally, so that it can be used by other classes and added to later.

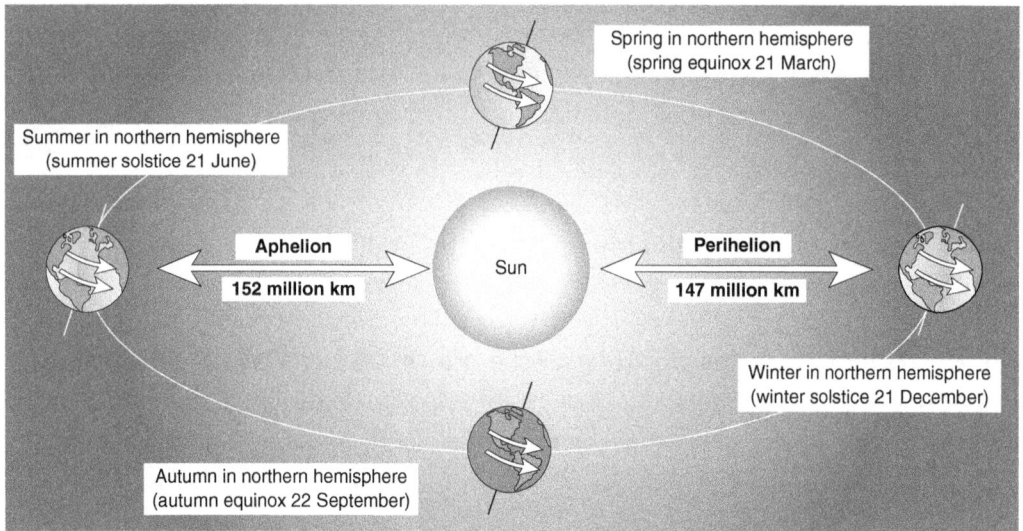

Figure 10.2 The seasons

Why do we get seasons?

The common misconception is that we are closer to the Sun in summer, which makes us hotter (Osbourne et al., 1994), but this isn't true. We're actually closest in spring and autumn due to the elliptical nature of the Earth's orbit around the Sun. The Earth's axis is tilted at an angle of 23.5°. It is this tilt that is the reason for the seasons by changing the angle at which sunlight hits the planet at different times of the year.

In December, the northern hemisphere is tilted away from the Sun and is in winter. The sunlight that reaches the northern hemisphere is weaker and colder because it is spread over a bigger area. In July, the northern hemisphere tilts towards the Sun and so is in summer, while the southern hemisphere tilts away from it. The sunlight that reaches the northern hemisphere is stronger and hotter because it is concentrated in a small area. The opposite is true for the southern hemisphere.

Countries on the Equator stay roughly at the same angle towards the Sun over the year, so they stay constant all year round.

As the Earth orbits the Sun, the days get longer and the nights become shorter for the hemisphere that is tilting towards the sun. At the halfway point, neither hemisphere is tilted towards or away from the Sun. The days and nights are (almost) equal length. This date is called the **Equinox** from the Latin *aequus* (equal) and *nox* (night).

For the northern hemisphere, the Spring Equinox is usually 20 March and the Autumn Equinox is usually 22 September.

North of the Arctic Circle, the Sun will not set throughout the entire summer, which is why it is called the Land of the Midnight Sun. At the Autumn Equinox, the Sun sinks below the horizon leading to twilight until early October. After that, the Sun never rises and the North Pole is in permanent darkness for the whole of the winter. This is also true for the Antarctic, but for the southern hemisphere it is winter/summer.

Why do we get phases of the Moon?

Over the course of a month, the Moon looks a little different each day. The changing shapes that the Moon appears to take are called **phases**. A complete cycle of phases is known as a lunar month. The Moon takes 27.3 days to make a complete orbit of the Earth, but because the Earth is also turning and moving around the Sun, there are actually 29.5 days from one new Moon to the next new Moon.

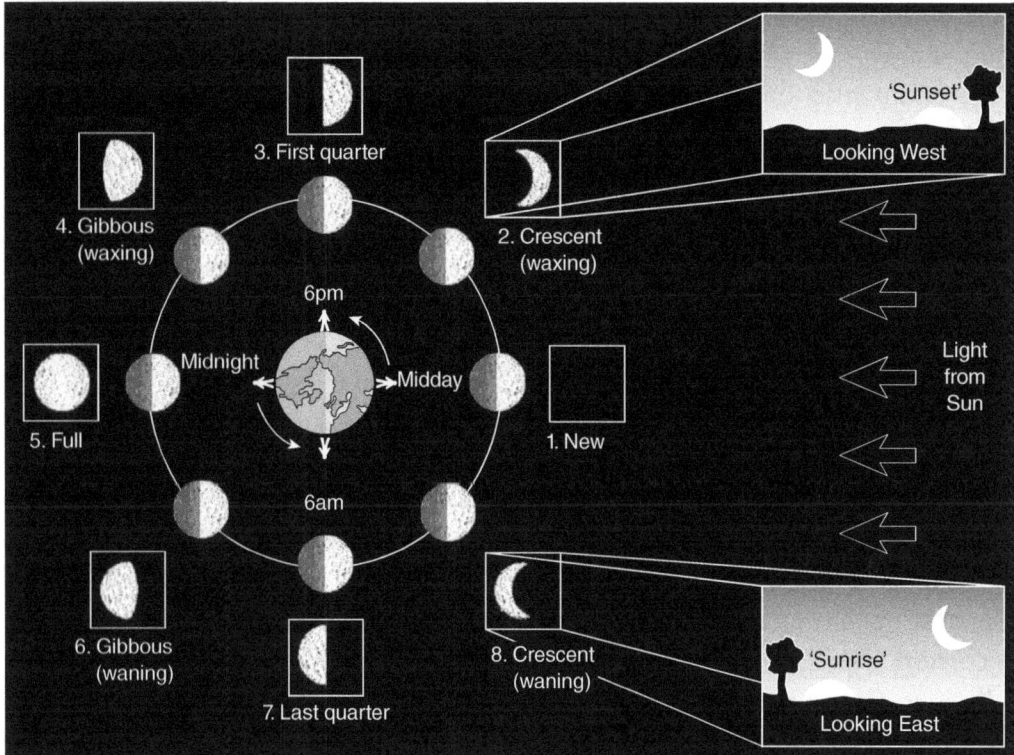

Figure 10.3 The phases of the Moon

A common misconception is that the phases of the Moon are caused by the Earth's shadow (Osbourne et al., 1994). In fact, these phases are caused by the relative position of the Moon as it orbits the Earth and how we see the Moon as it is being lit from the Sun.

In the same way that we get day and night on Earth, the Moon is lit in the same way. Half the Moon is in bright sunlight and the other half is in darkness. As the Moon orbits the Earth, we see different proportions of light and dark parts of the Moon.

When the Earth is between the Sun and the Moon, we see a Full Moon. This is because the whole face of the Moon reflecting the sunlight is facing us. We see none of the dark face because it is pointing away from the Earth.

When the Moon is a quarter of a way further round in its orbit, we see half of the dark face and half of the light face. We see a Half Moon (Third Quarter Moon). When the Moon moves between the Sun and the Earth, we see no Moon at all, as the side reflecting sunlight is facing away from the Earth. This is called a New Moon.

You can model this in the classroom with a torch and a ball or you could use a ball with one half painted black. Change the position that you see the ball (move round in a circle with the ball in the middle) and draw the phases of the Moon that you see.

There are also online simulations you can use (see the Further reading and resources section at the end of this chapter for details).

Stars, planets and galaxies

Our Sun is actually a **star**. It is the same as all the stars we see in the night sky, but it is much closer, which is why it looks bigger in the sky. A star is a massive ball of extremely hot, luminous gas (plasma) that is held together by its own gravity. In fact, our Sun is a rather small star compared to many other stars in the sky. Polaris, the Pole Star, is around 50 times larger than our sun.

Orbiting the Sun are **planets**. These are large round balls of rock or gas. Some of these planets have **moons** that orbit them.

Also orbiting our Sun are smaller balls of rock that are not quite planets, called **dwarf planets**. There are also smaller lumps of rock called **asteroids** and balls of ice known as **comets**. The Sun, plus all these objects orbiting it are called a **solar system.**

A group of stars is known as a **galaxy**. The galaxy that we are a part of is called the Milky Way. It contains around 100 billion stars in a disc that is over 100,000 light years wide.

The solar system

A **solar system** is the name given to a star with planets orbiting around it. For us, it's the eight planets that orbit our Sun, along with dwarf planets and asteroids.

The eight planets are:

- Mercury
- Venus
- Earth
- Mars
- Jupiter
- Saturn
- Uranus
- Neptune.

Mercury, Venus, Earth and Mars are rocky planets. Jupiter, Saturn, Uranus and Neptune are known as 'gas giants'.

Orbiting some of these planets are moons. Mars has two moons. Jupiter has 67 moons. Saturn has 53 named moons, as well as an amazing ring system. Did you know that Jupiter, Uranus and Neptune also have rings?

One of the best places to find out about all the planets and dwarf planets is the NASA solar system website.

Why is Pluto not a planet?

When it was first discovered in 1930, Pluto was considered to be a planet. However, as our telescopes became more accurate, more objects were discovered that were larger than Pluto and there needed to be an agreement about which objects were classed as planets and which were not. In 2006, the International Astronomical Union decided on a definition of a planet.

To be a planet, the following criteria had to be met:

- To orbit the Sun (so therefore not a moon).
- To be massive enough for gravity to shape it (make it round).
- To have cleared its orbit of all other objects.

Pluto has not cleared its orbit of other objects – it shares its orbit with other large lumps of rock and ice. Pluto was therefore demoted from being a planet and reclassified as a dwarf planet. However, as there is a lot of contention around this definition of a planet, Pluto may yet be reinstated.

At the time of writing, there are five agreed dwarf planets:

- Ceres
- Pluto
- Haumea
- Makemake
- Eris.

Challenges and misconceptions the children may have

A common misconception that children have is the idea that the Earth is fixed and the Sun moves around us (Osbourne et al., 1994). It's easy to come to that conclusion since from our point of view we appear stationary and the Sun seems to move across the sky.

The Earth is spinning at around 1600km/h while also moving through space around the Sun at roughly 107,000 km/h. For many people, the idea that the Earth is moving so quickly is very challenging as you can't feel the movement. We can see the effects of the Earth spinning – the Sun appears to move in the sky every day because of our spin and the stars rotate around us over the course of a night.

There is no such thing as 'the dark side of the Moon', a face of the Moon that never sees sunlight. As the Moon rotates and orbits the Earth, the entire surface of the Moon gets an equal amount of sunlight and darkness. There is, however, a far side of the Moon that we never see from Earth. The Moon rotates as it orbits the Earth so that the same face is always pointing towards the Earth.

Children (and sadly, some adults) might think that the Earth is flat. Use models and globes as well as images of the Earth from space to show that the Earth is a sphere. Explain that gravity pulls everything towards the centre of the Earth, so someone in the UK will be pulled towards the centre, just as someone standing on the Equator or someone in Australia would be.

Making the learning real: linking the unit to everyday life

In KS1, the children should already have an understanding that the weather changes through the course of a year. They should know about times of the year when it is hot and sunny, and times when it is cold and snowy. Some may have relatives who live overseas (or have lived overseas themselves) and might know that some countries have very hot weather at Christmas.

In KS2, Space is a topic area that many children will already have an interest in and will perhaps already know a lot about. Some may already have favourite books about space, which they could bring in and talk about. Draw on this expertise and enthusiasm. Try to channel their natural curiosity.

Children are likely to have seen films and television shows about space and aliens. These could be used to start a topic on space or as a discussion starter. Ask the children to discuss which parts of the film or show they think could really happen, and which parts are made up.

Practical lesson ideas

Watch your shadows

Go into the playground first thing in the morning on a sunny day. Working in pairs, each child uses chalk to draw a cross on the ground, then stands on the cross while their partner draws around their shadow. Repeat this several times through the school day. Describe how their shadows change. Use digital cameras or iPads to record their evidence.

Note: children should be warned that it is not safe to look directly at the Sun, even when wearing dark glasses.

Weather charts

Make a table to record the weather. This could be carried out every day or one day a week through the year. Measure temperature and what the weather is like. This could be presented as a chart on a class display and could include photographs.

Solar system models

Many different guides are available to help you model the solar system on a playground or school field. Some also scale the size of the planets, while others keep them large to make it easier to see. Schoolyard Solar System, Solar System in My Pocket and Toilet Roll Solar System are all worth exploring (full details can be found in the Further reading and resources section at end of this chapter).

A computer simulation such as Solar System Scope would also be a good tool to allow the pupils to explore how the planets move in relation to the Sun and to each other. The children could use it to work out the length of a year on different planets.

Model Sun, Moon and Earth

The children could create a paper model that demonstrates the motion of the Sun, Moon and Earth. Use three discs (large, medium and small) and two strips of card. Fix them with paper fasteners. The Moon should be able to rotate around the Earth and the Earth (with the Moon) can rotate around the Sun.

Sustainability links

There may not be any direct curriculum links between the movement of the Earth, Moon and Sun to the Sustainable Development goals, but there are plenty of ways the broader topic of Space could be linked to them. Satellites orbiting the Earth are used to monitor many things, such as crops, air quality, polar ice cover and water quality, linking to goals such as Climate Action, Zero Hunger and Clean Water. Visit the websites of space organisations such as NASA and the ESA for more information.

Cross-curricular links and opportunities

KS1

The Seasonal Changes topic provides many data handling and numeracy opportunities, including collecting and looking at data on day lengths and time differences around the world.

There are a great many religious festivals associated with the changing seasons. Christmas, Hanukkah and Diwali are all midwinter festivals associated with lights, when the nights are long.

In Art and Design, the children could create paintings and drawings inspired by the colours of the different seasons. They could collect leaves in autumn and make pictures from leaf prints.

KS2

In KS2, there are plenty of opportunities to make cross-curricular links with music, art and storytelling. The children could create music or movement pieces to represent each of the planets in the solar system. They could create paintings or models of the planets, the night sky or the solar system.

The children could research some of the different constellations and find out some of the stories and legends behind them. They could then re-create some of the main constellations such as Orion or the Plough using glow-in-the-dark stars, or by making pinholes in sheets of black paper and sticking them on the windows. This could even link to history and geography by finding out how sailors used to navigate using the stars or how Stonehenge or the Pyramids were aligned with the Sun and the stars.

Progression

The children start by exploring and describing the seasons and then in Year 5 try to explain why we get them. They could also describe the movement of the Sun, Earth and Moon, and explain why the Sun appears to move across the sky every day. This links to the Year 5 Forces unit where the children will look at gravity.

Suggested scientists

A great many space scientists could be featured here who children might like to research. Some examples include:

- **Helen Sharman** First British person to go into space. Spent seven days as a cosmonaut on the Russian Mir space station in 1991.
- **Katherine Johnson** NASA mathematician whose calculations of orbital mechanics were critical in getting the Apollo spacecraft to the Moon and back safely.
- **Mae Jemison** First Black female astronaut to go into space. Served on the Space Shuttle *Endeavour* for eight days in September 1992.
- **Caroline Herschel** First woman to discover a comet. Assisted her brother in discovering Uranus.
- **Ibn al-Haytham (Alhazen)** Islamic scholar who made many discoveries in optics, mathematics and astronomy. He further developed the geocentric model.

Further reading and resources

Cary Huang – The Scale of the Universe: https://htwins.net/scale2/

Institute of Physics (IOP) – Toilet Roll Solar System: www.iop.org/explore-physics/at-home/episode-11-toilet-roll-solar-system#gref

Lunar Phase Simulator: https://ccnmtl.github.io/astro-simulations/lunar-phase-simulator/

NASA – Solar System Exploration: https://solarsystem.nasa.gov/

The Ogden Trust – Solar System in my Pocket: www.ogdentrust.com/resources/phizzi-practical-solar-system-in-my-pocket

Schoolyard Solar System: https://nssdc.gsfc.nasa.gov/planetary/education/schoolyard_ss/

Science Fix – Sun, Earth and Moon Papercraft Model: www.sciencefix.co.uk/2019/07/quick-science-idea-sun-earth-and-moon-papercraft-model/

Solar System Scope: www.solarsystemscope.com/

CHAPTER 11

Electricity

Introduction

It is hard to imagine our modern world without electricity. It is all around us, powering our lights, heating and much of our entertainment. To most of us, life would be unthinkable without electricity.

The Ancient Greeks knew that some objects, such as amber, could be rubbed with fur to pick up light objects such as feathers, and we get the word electricity from the Greek word for amber, *elektron*.

Science knowledge you need before you can teach this topic

What is electricity?

Electricity can be thought of as the flow of tiny, charged particles called electrons. The size of the flow is called the **current**. The pupils can think of it like water flowing down a river – the faster the flow of water, the bigger the current.

At primary level, the explanation for electricity needs to be simplified from the one used in KS3 and above. Electrons are not introduced to pupils until Year 10. So, for primary it might be wise to talk about small particles that carry something called **'charge'** (Chapman, 2014). These charged particles moving around the wires produce electricity. If you have introduced the idea of tiny particles in Year 4 Solids, Liquids and Gases unit, and also in the Sound unit, this can be linked to those ideas.

Electricity can only flow when a power supply is able to 'push' the electrons around a complete circuit. This means that a path is needed from the power supply, through the components in the circuit, and back to the power supply. The size of the push is called the **voltage**. The higher the voltage, the bigger the push moving the electrons around the circuit.

Electricity is a form of energy. It can be converted by circuit components, such as light bulbs, motors and buzzers, into other useful forms of energy.

Circuits

For electricity to flow, a complete circuit is needed. If there is a gap in the circuit, electricity won't flow.

Series circuits

The simplest type of circuit is known as a **series circuit**. In this type of circuit, each component is connected in a single loop one after the other, so the current has to pass through each in turn and is the same at every point in the circuit.

One disadvantage of this type of circuit is that if one component fails, it will create a gap in the circuit and current will not flow through the rest of the components. This would create a problem if, for example, bulbs were connected in series. Old Christmas tree lights used to be connected together in this way. If one bulb were to fail, the others would also switch off. Similarly, each of the bulbs could not be controlled individually as a switch would stop current flowing in the entire circuit.

A **short circuit** is a path in a circuit that contains no components. In a short circuit, there is very little resistance to the flow of electricity and therefore the current will take this path around the circuit.

Parallel circuits are when the components are connected in more than one loop. Switches are able to switch one light on or off and not affect any others. This is how most of your house is wired up. There is no requirement to understand these in the primary national curriculum.

Conductors and insulators

A conductor is a material that allows energy (heat or electricity) to pass through it easily. All metals are good conductors because their electrons are free to move from one atom to the next and take the energy with them. Wires are often made of copper because it is a good conductor of electricity.

An insulator is a material that does not allow electricity or heat to pass through it easily. The electrons in insulators are not free to move or to carry energy from one atom to the next. Rubber, plastic and wood are all insulators.

Children can investigate different materials by putting them into a simple series circuit between two crocodile clips and seeing if a light bulb comes on or not.

One common non-metal that is a conductor is graphite. The 'lead' from a pencil (which is actually graphite) will conduct electricity. Sharpen both ends of a pencil to make it easier to attach the clips.

Bulbs and batteries

When you add more light bulbs to a series circuit, the brightness of the bulbs should decrease. This is because the battery provides a specific amount of energy to the electrons linked to the voltage of the battery. As the electrons flow around a circuit, they provide the components with electrical energy and the bulbs convert this electrical energy into light (and heat) energy.

The available energy is shared between all the components. The more bulbs there are in the circuit, the less energy is available for each one, and the dimmer the bulbs become.

Changing the voltage of the battery (or adding more batteries) also affects the brightness of the bulbs. As the voltage increases, the energy provided to the electrons also increases. The larger the amount of electrical energy supplied, the brighter the bulbs will be.

Devices that use electricity

There are many devices in the classroom and in our homes that use electricity. Some use mains electricity and some run on batteries. Children should be able to group devices into those that use batteries, those that use mains electricity and those that use both.

It can be a little tricky for children to differentiate them these days, since many of their toys and gadgets use a rechargeable battery and can run on both mains or battery, such as phones, tablets, digital cameras and laptops. Include obvious items such as a fridge, TV, washing machine and lights.

Sustainability link

Children can think about the way we use electricity and the need to conserve energy. How much electricity does the school (or their home) use in a normal day and what measures could be taken to reduce this electricity use? They could research batteries and how scientists are trying to develop better batteries for electric cars. What are the environmental problems caused by mining raw materials to use in batteries, and what can we do to minimise them?

Drawing circuits

In Year 4, the pupils are expected to simply draw circuits as they appear in real life – with wiggly wires and batteries and bulbs drawn how they are. In Year 6, the pupils would be expected to draw circuits using the more scientific symbols and straight lines.

The basic symbols they are expected to draw are as follows.

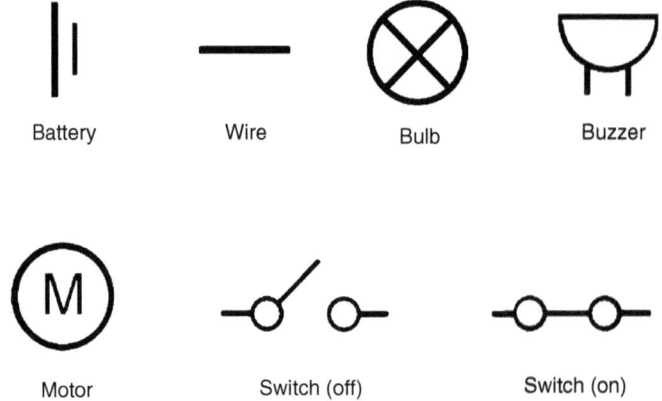

Battery   Wire   Bulb   Buzzer

Motor   Switch (off)   Switch (on)

Figure 11.1   Basic electrical symbols

To help with the transition, Chapman (2014) suggests building real circuits on a large sheet of sugar paper alongside the circuit diagram, so pupils can see how the real circuit relates to the diagram.

Models and analogies in electricity

Electricity is a tricky topic to teach because it is an abstract concept. We can see its effect on something like a light bulb, but it is very hard to explain what is actually happening inside a circuit, particularly at primary school level. When asked to draw what is going on inside a wire, children often draw waves or sparks (Kibble, 2002).

To help understand what is going on, it can be helpful to use a model or an analogy, bringing in a different frame of reference to help describe what is happening. For example, many people think about electricity in terms of something else – water flowing through pipes or traffic moving along roads (Asoko, 1995).

For more on models and analogies in science, see Chapter 1.

No model is perfect. They will usually fall down on some aspect of what actually happens inside a circuit, but the shortfalls could be discussed with the pupils.

Here are a few suggestions for models that could be used.

Water pump

Imagine that the wires are pipes and filled with water. The pump is the battery that pushes the water around the pipes. The water mimics the flow of electricity, which we call current. The strength of the pump is the voltage – the bigger the push, the faster the water flows around the pipes and the bigger the current.

A water wheel represents a component such as a bulb. The faster the current, the faster the water wheel moves (the brighter the bulb).

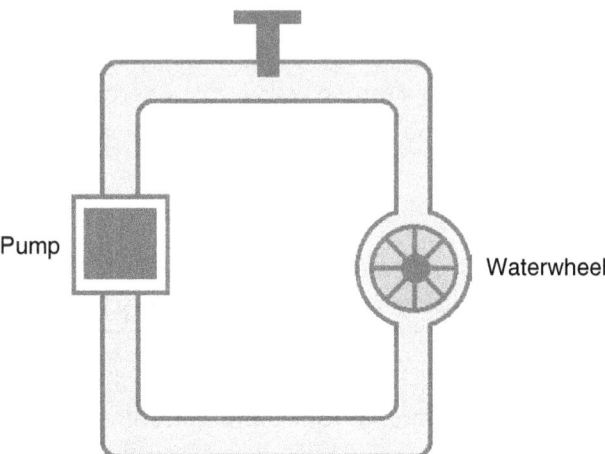

Figure 11.2 A waterwheel model of a circuit

String loop model

Use a small group of pupils and ask them to sit in a circle on the floor. Use a loop of string (or a hoop) to play the role of the electrons inside the wire. Ask the children to hold their hands out so that the string can pass between their thumb and forefinger. One child can then act as the battery and they start moving the string (electrons) around the circle. The movement of the string is the current, flowing around in a circuit.

Care needs to be taken with this model to avoid giving the misconception that it is the wire that is moving.

The IOP website has some more examples of models that can be used (see website details in the Further reading and resources section at the end of the chapter).

Electrical safety

It is important to take precautions when using electricity and teach children about the dangers. Children should be taught never to touch exposed wires. They should never leave liquids next to electrical appliances or operate with wet hands. Always switch lights off at the mains before changing light bulbs. Switch off all electrical appliances before you leave the house or go to bed.

Explain the dangers of overhead power lines: be careful when flying kites or climbing trees near power lines, or when carrying long fishing lines. They should be warned about going near transformers in electrical substations or electrified railway lines.

Sustainability link

Children could find out about green ways to generate electricity. Does the school have solar panels? Could they design a green school that generates its own renewable energy?

Challenges and misconceptions the children may have

A common misconception is that children believe that the current is used up as it travels around the circuit, and that there is more current in the wire before the bulb and less current in the wire after the bulb. In reality, there is the same current at every point in the circuit.

The nature of electricity in the wires is hard to visualise, with children imagining that inside the wire there are sparks or waves passing through it.

If the battery supplies electricity to the bulb to make it work, why is there a need for a second wire to connect back to the battery? Also, if the electricity goes round in a circuit and comes back to the battery, why does it go flat (Asoko, 2002)?

Making the learning real: linking the unit to everyday life

Children will have regular experiences with electricity every day of their lives. They will know that televisions and games consoles will not work unless they are plugged in. Many toys need batteries to work, and children should be aware that batteries come in all different shapes and sizes. Batteries are a good introduction to voltage and the size of the 'push' around a circuit.

Children may know that many cars now run on electricity – their parents may even have one. Why might this be good for the environment?

Most children will know that phones and tablet computers in the home need charging from time to time. They may know that there are batteries inside and that they need to be plugged into the mains to recharge.

Practical lesson ideas

Energy Sticks

An Energy Stick is an excellent gadget for teaching circuits in primary schools. It is relatively inexpensive and you just need one to use with a whole class to make an impact. Use it to turn the whole class into a circuit by holding hands. When the circuit is complete, it buzzes.

Electrical audit

Carry out a survey in the classroom. Make a list of all the devices that use electricity. Divide them into groups – those that use mains electricity, those that use batteries and those that have both. The children could carry out a similar task at home.

Making switches

Give the children a square of card, two paper fasteners and either some tin foil or a paperclip. Ask them to make a working switch that they could put into a simple series circuit to turn a small bulb on and off.

Batteries

Select a range of small toys that use different types of batteries. Ask the children to take the batteries out of the toys and look at their different shapes and sizes. Put the toys into groups according to the types of batteries they use. Record the results as a graph or pictogram. (Safety precaution: take care with small batteries and warn the children not to put them in their mouth.)

Application of electricity: things to make and do

As stated in the national curriculum, Year 6 builds on the work completed in Year 4: 'Pupils should construct simple series circuits, to help them to answer questions about what happens when they try different components, for example, switches, bulbs, buzzers and motors.'

Pupils should also be able to use their knowledge to design and make useful circuits. They could build a simple model of a windmill using a motor to spin cardboard blades. This will provide opportunities for cross-curricular links to Design and Technology.

These useful circuits all allow the pupils to apply their knowledge of circuits to design different things.

Here are some examples, you can find links at the end of the unit.

- Burglar alarm
- Buzz Wire Game
- Game of Operation
- Paper circuits
- Traffic lights.

Telegraphs and Morse Code

Imagine a circuit with a simple switch and a buzzer. When the switch is closed, the buzzer sounds. Now imagine that this circuit is really long – the switch is in one town and the buzzer is in another town. That's basically how the telegraph system worked in the 1840s. Using Morse Code, messages could be sent, letter by letter, much faster than via the postal service. Wires were even laid under the Atlantic to allow messages to be sent from Europe to America.

Pupils could explore Morse Code and send simple messages to each other. This would link nicely to a topic on The Victorians or Codebreaking.

Cross-curricular links and opportunities

This topic area can link with Design and Technology to create different objects that contain simple circuits as outlined above. The children could use copper tape which, along with LED bulbs and pin batteries, could be used to make flashing paper Christmas trees or greetings cards.

In history, the children could find out about what life was like before we had electricity and consider how we managed without constant hot water and instant lights. They could research the story of how electricity was discovered and the roles of people such as Allesandro Volta and Luigi Galvani. They could look at how the telegraph revolutionised communication in Victorian times.

In geography, the children could explore how remote villages and towns generate electricity, finding out about renewable energy sources such as solar panels and wind turbines.

Progression

In KS1, materials that are able to conduct electricity is a topic that could be explored. The children can progress from drawing diagrams of the circuits as they appear in real life to drawing diagrams with straight lines and symbols for components. They then move from describing how an electrical circuit behaves to explaining reasons why it behaves the way it does. Children can then apply their knowledge of circuits to building circuits that perform different roles.

Suggested scientists

Many electrical scientists could be featured here who children might like to research. Some examples include:

- **Joseph Swan** British physicist and chemist who independently invented an incandescent light bulb.

(Continued)

- **Nikola Tesla** Serbian-American inventor and electrical engineer. A pioneer in the development of alternating current (AC) electrical systems and numerous other ground-breaking inventions.
- **Edith Clarke** First ever female American electrical engineer. Made pioneering advancements in power system analysis and the development of graphical calculators.
- **Hertha Marks Ayrton** British physicist and engineer. First female member of the Institution of Electrical Engineers.

Further reading and resources

Burglar alarm: www.electronics-notes.com/articles/basic_concepts/stem-projects-activities/how-to-build-burglar-alarm.php

Buzz Wire Game: www.instructables.com/id/Buzz-Wire-Kit/

Electrical safety in the home: www.switchedonkids.org.uk/electrical-safety-in-your-home

Giant Game of Operation: www.instructables.com/id/Giant-Game-of-Operation/

IOP: Electric circuit models: www.iop.org/sites/default/files/2019-11/Electric-circuits.ppt

IOP: The rope loop model of a circuit: https://spark.iop.org/rope-loop-electric-circuit-model

IOP: Spark – Energy: https://spark.iop.org/collections/energy-new-curriculum

Nicholson, D. (2019) 'Teaching Circuits with an Energy Stick': www.sciencefix.co.uk/2019/05/teaching-circuits-with-an-energy-stick/

Paper Circuits: www.exploratorium.edu/tinkering/projects/paper-circuits

Scrappy Circuits: https://makezine.com/projects/scrappy-circuits/

Squishy Circuits: https://squishycircuits.com/

CHAPTER 12

Light and Sound

Introduction

Light is vitally important to us all. From the moment we wake up, we are making use of light to see the world around us. The light from the Sun travels millions of miles through space to reach us, bathing our planet in energy that is locked into all the food that we eat and the fuels that we burn.

Sound, too, is very important to us. Through speech, we create sounds to communicate with others. We express our personalities through the music that we listen to or that we make.

Sight and hearing are two of the most important senses by which most of us are able to explore the world around us and communicate with each other. The teaching of light and sound can also provide great cross-curricular links between science, music and art, and allow the children to express themselves creatively in different ways.

Science knowledge you need before you can teach this topic

What is light?

Light is a form of energy. Visible light refers to the section of the electromagnetic spectrum that can be seen by a typical human eye. Other forms of electromagnetic radiation include infrared, ultraviolet, radio waves, microwaves and X-rays. All these forms of radiation travel as waves.

Unlike sound waves, electromagnetic waves do not need to be transferred via molecules or atoms, and so are able to travel through a vacuum. This is why light from the Sun is able to reach the Earth through the vacuum of space. It takes around 8 minutes for light to travel from the Sun to the Earth.

White light is light that appears colourless to the eye. It is produced by natural light sources like the Sun and artificial light sources such as light bulbs. White light is made up of a spectrum of colours with different wavelengths: red, orange, yellow, green, blue, indigo and violet.

Light vs. sound

Light is incredibly fast, travelling at 300,000 km/s. By comparison, sound is very slow at about 330m/s in the air. Light can travel through a vacuum, whereas sound cannot. If it was actually possible for sound to travel through a vacuum, it has been calculated that the Sun would be constantly blaring out a noise of about 100 decibels! If the Sun were to vanish, it would take 8 minutes for the light to stop reaching us and for it to become dark and cold. We would, however, keep hearing that 100-decibel roar for another 14 years!

Exploring light and sound in EYFS

Young pupils can explore light and sound as part of using their senses, and this can provide engaging and stimulating sensory experiences. Pupils could use a light table or an overhead projector to explore making patterns from different translucent objects such as plastic tiles, glass pebbles and acrylic shapes. They could use simple musical instruments such as toy drums, shakers and xylophones to explore making different sounds.

The teaching of light and sound can also provide great cross-curricular links with art and music, and allow the pupils to express themselves creatively in different ways.

Light sources

A light source is anything that gives out or emits light. This can include natural sources such as the Sun and fire, but will also include artificial sources such as light bulbs and various device screens.

Bioluminescence is an interesting feature of some living things, such as fireflies and jellyfish, which are able to produce light as a result of chemical reactions inside their bodies.

Most other objects reflect light, which is how we are able to see them. Children often misidentify shiny objects such as mirrors and metals, and think they are light sources. The Moon reflects the light of the Sun, but is not a source of light.

How do we see?

We are able to see things because light rays bounce off objects and into our eyes. The light that bounces off a surface is called 'reflected light'. Light that is not reflected by objects is absorbed.

Coloured materials reflect some wavelengths of the light and absorb others. White materials reflect all the colours of light. Black materials absorb all the colours of light.

When asked to explain how we see things, pupils may draw arrows coming out of a person's eyes and hitting objects (SPACE, 1990a). Vision is seen as an active process where we are scanning for objects. We see because light from a light source bounces off objects and enters our eyes.

How does the eye work?

The eye consists of five key parts. Light enters the eye through a protective, transparent covering, called the **cornea**. This helps bend the light into the round hole in the centre of the eye, called the **pupil**.

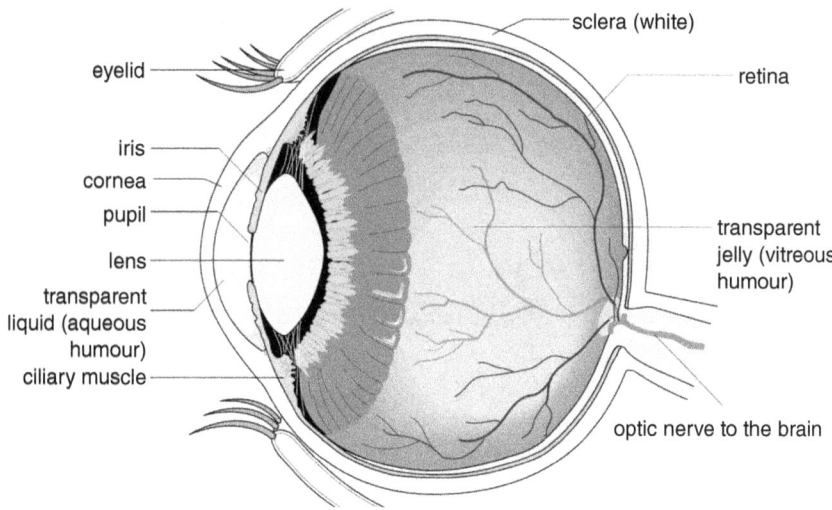

Figure 12.1   The human eye

Surrounding the pupil is the coloured part of the eye, called the **iris**. The iris can expand or contract to change the size of the pupil, depending on how bright or dark it is.

Immediately behind the iris is the **lens**. This focuses the light onto the thin layer of tissue at the back of the eyeball, called the **retina**.

The retina contains over 100 million light-sensing cells. There are two main types of light- sensing cell – **rods** and **cones**. The rod cells only see in black and white. They provide peripheral vision, allow us to detect motion and help us see in dim light. The cone cells are larger and work better in bright light. They allow us to see in colour and help us to focus. As light falls on the retina's light-sensing cells, it is converted into electrical impulses that pass along the optic nerve to the brain.

Note

Carrots *do not* make you see in the dark. This myth was spread during the Second World War by the British to hide the fact that they had invented radar and had become good at shooting down enemy planes at night.

Light travels in straight lines

Light travels in a straight line. We can demonstrate this by using three pieces of card with holes punched in the centre. Line them up so that when you shine a torch through the holes, you can see the spot of light on a screen or sheet of paper. If you

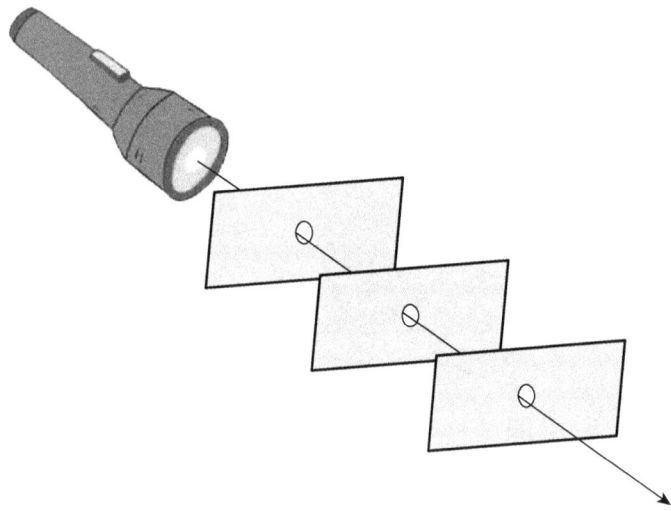

Figure 12.2   How light travels in straight lines

move the middle card left or right a few centimetres, then the spot vanishes. The light can't bend around to move through all the holes – it can only travel through when they're all lined up.

Mirrors

Reflection occurs when light bounces off a surface. All objects reflect at least some light. Shiny, smooth surfaces reflect lots of light in one direction and are known as reflectors. Other objects with uneven surfaces scatter light in many different directions and appear dull.

When a ray of light is reflected by a surface, the angle between the reflected ray and a line perpendicular to the surface at the point of reflection is known as the angle of reflection. The angle at which light strikes the surface is called the angle of incidence. These two angles should be exactly the same when light strikes a smooth surface such as a mirror.

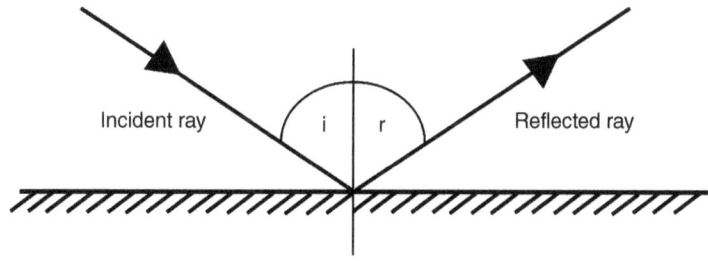

Figure 12.3   How light is reflected on a mirror

We can explore this to build objects like periscopes or kaleidoscopes using small mirrors and cardboard tubes.

How do we get shadows and how do they change?

When an object blocks the path of a beam of light, a shadow is formed. Because light travels in straight lines, it cannot bend around an object in its path, so a dark area is produced which has the same shape as the object.

The size of a shadow depends on the distance between the light source and the object that is creating the shadow. When the light source is close to the object, a lot of light is blocked and a large shadow is formed. When the object is far away, a smaller amount of light is blocked, so a smaller shadow is formed.

Opaque objects create dark shadows because they block all the light. Translucent objects, such as leaves, let a little light through so their shadows are not as dark as those created by opaque objects. Transparent objects, like water, let all light through and don't make any shadows at all.

Measuring light intensity

A light meter can be used to measure light intensity. They are often used by photographers to determine the amount of light available so that the most appropriate lens is used. The unit of measurement for light intensity is the lux (lx).

The children can use a light meter or a data logger with a light sensor to measure the light intensity of different light sources in the classroom. It is possible to do this using the camera of a tablet or phone using an app such as Arduino Science Journal or Phyphox.

They could measure light intensity from various light sources. They should observe that as they move further away from a light source, light intensity decreases. This is because the light energy becomes spread out over an increasingly large area.

Sustainability link

The children could explore how to use light to generate electricity. They could look at different solar-powered toys. Research if solar panels still work on cloudy days.

What is sound?

Sound is produced when something vibrates, like a guitar string or a loudspeaker. This makes the particles in the air vibrate, which makes the particles next to them vibrate, and so on. The sound wave spreads out as a ripple of vibrations, in the same way as ripples in a pond spread out when a stone is dropped into it (SPACE, 1990b).

Sound waves need a medium such as air, wood or water through which to travel. They cannot travel through a vacuum because there are no particles to pass on the energy. As the poster for *Alien* said, 'In space, no one can hear you scream.' In reality, every space battle you see in the movies should be totally silent, as there is no air to carry the sound of the lasers and explosions, but a silent space battle would be boring, so they don't do it!

Travelling sounds

Sound waves carry energy from one place to another by moving the medium they travel through. The waves move the medium as a series of **compressions** where the molecules move together and **rarefactions** where they are spread further apart. The energy travels in the same direction as the movement of the wave. This is called a **longitudinal** wave. In comparison, light travels as a **transverse** wave – it moves side to side perpendicular to the direction of travel.

Investigating sound: changing pitch and volume

To make sound waves easier for us to visualise, they are often drawn as a sine wave, like a light wave or ocean wave. The forward/back movement of the wave is converted into an up/down curve instead.

The distance from peak to peak is called the **wavelength**. The height is called the **amplitude**.

While it is easier to draw them like this, it is important not to mix this up with the way that the sound waves move.

The **pitch** of a sound refers to whether it is perceived as high or low in tone. Pitch depends on the frequency of the vibrations. Imagine you are standing in one spot and can see the waves passing by. The **frequency** of a sound is the number of waves that pass by in one second. So, if ten waves pass by, the frequency is 10Hz. If 100 waves pass, by the frequency is 100Hz.

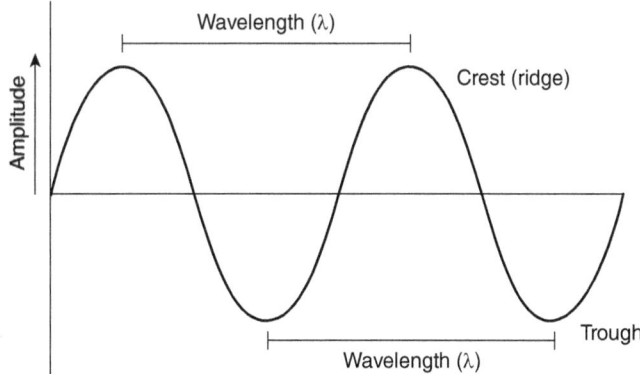

Figure 12.4   The features of a wave

Source: High School Earth Science, Wikibook, CC BY-SA 3.0

Exploring pitch

Musicians change the pitch of their instruments in different ways. The strings of an instrument such as a guitar can be tuned by changing their tension. Tightening makes them vibrate at a higher frequency, creating a higher pitched note, while loosening the strings creates a lower pitched note. By moving their finger along a guitar string, a guitarist can effectively make the vibrating section of string longer or shorter. Shorter strings vibrate faster than longer strings, so the pitch of the note changes. Also, plucking each of the strings will produce a different note; the thicker strings vibrate slower and produce lower notes than the thinner strings.

In wind instruments, the length and volume of the air column will affect the pitch. This can be altered by covering the holes along the instrument.

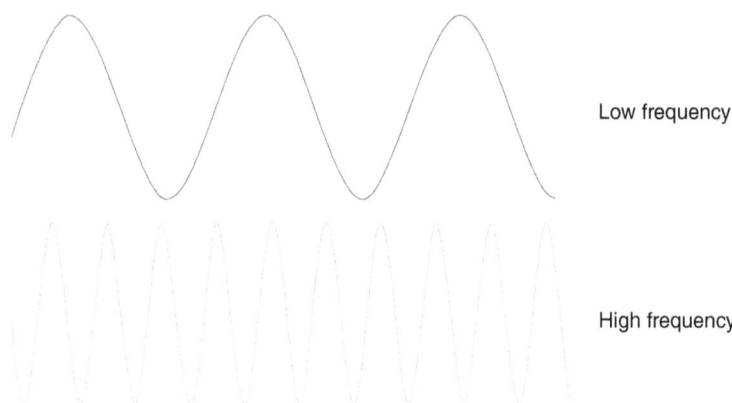

Figure 12.5   High frequency vs. low frequency

Hang a ruler over the edge of a desk. Change how much of the ruler is hanging over the edge. Experiment and see what happens. The longer the length of ruler hanging over the edge, the slower it will vibrate and the lower the note.

Amplitude and volume

The amplitude of the wave is how far it vibrates forwards and backwards. On a graph, it can be shown as the distance from the midpoint to the top of the wave.

In a quiet sound, the amplitude is small. The wave doesn't move much and has a small amount of energy. In a loud sound, the amplitude is high. The wave moves a lot and has a large amount of energy.

A bigger vibration, caused by plucking a string, blowing or hitting an object with greater intensity, increases the volume. The larger the vibration, the more energy it has and the louder the sound.

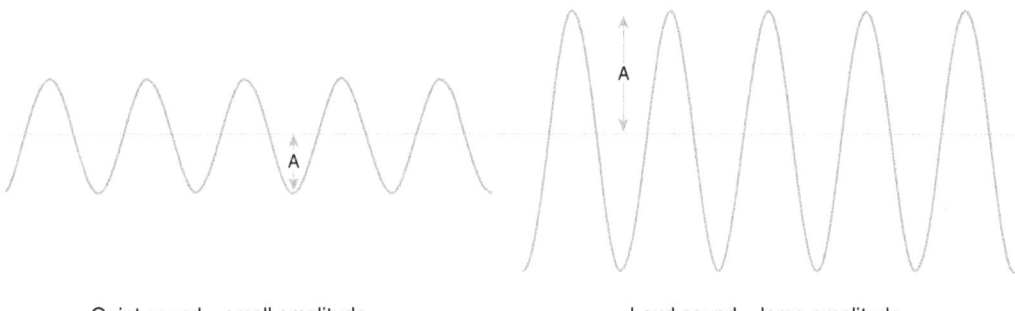

Quiet sound – small amplitude   Loud sound – large amplitude

Figure 12.6   Loud sounds vs. quiet sounds

How do we hear?

The vibrations in the air reach us and are gathered by our outer ear. The sound is funnelled down the ear canal and makes the eardrum vibrate.

The vibrations are then transferred via three small bones called the ossicles to the cochlea. The cochlea is filled with liquid and nerve cells. The vibrations in the liquid are picked up by these hair cells and sent as impulses along the auditory nerve to the brain, which translates the messages into a sensation of sound.

Challenges and misconceptions the children may have

Children often think that light is only found in bright places. They know that dark is the opposite of light, so assume that if it is dark, there must not be any light around at all. In reality, even on a dark night there will always be some light present. If you have thick curtains, black out the classroom and ask the children what they can see once their eyes have adjusted to the dark.

When asked to explain how we see things, children may draw arrows coming out of a person's eyes and hitting objects. Really, it is the opposite way around: light travels from the light source to the objects and then into our eyes.

Children have some interesting concepts about the nature of sound. Some might think that the sound is only present inside their ears or that the listener has to be concentrating on the sound source for the sound to be heard. Explain to children that sounds are made by objects that vibrate, and that those vibrations make the air vibrate, which carries the sound to their ears.

When asked to show how sound travels from an object such as a bell to our ears, the children might draw sounds travelling as musical notes, probably having seen similar in comics or cartoons. Children might think that sounds travel in straight lines, from the sound source to their ears. This is probably as a result of having taught them that light travels in this way. To demonstrate how the vibrations move out in all directions, use a flat tray of water and drop a small pebble into it. They can see the waves moving out in a circle.

Making the learning real: linking the unit to everyday life

In order to embed the concepts of light, you can relate this topic area to real-world examples and experiences that are familiar to the children. Do any of the children in your class wear glasses? Do they understand how their glasses work? Glasses help people to see by bending light and focusing it onto the back of the eye.

Children will know that they can see their reflection in a mirror, but they probably won't have given any thought to how mirrors actually work. The children might wear reflective clothing when walking to school or riding their bicycles, so this could be used as an introduction to the concept of reflected light.

Use musical instruments as a way to introduce the children to the idea of how different sounds are made. See if there are any musical instruments in the school that could be used in these lessons to investigate sounds and vibrations.

As an easy demonstration, you can ask students to talk with their hand touching their throat. Ask them if they can they feel the vibrations as they speak.

Do any of your students wear a hearing aid? Do they know how one helps them to hear? Hearing aids often amplify the sounds that are difficult to hear. They work on the sounds coming into our ears rather than the other way around.

Practical lesson ideas

Light tables

Children could use a light table or an overhead projector to explore making patterns from different translucent objects such as plastic tiles, glass pebbles and acrylic shapes. A cheap light table can be made from a plastic storage box with white Christmas tree lights inside.

Blackout tents

Make a blackout den from thick fabric and a desk, or buy a pop-up sensory black-out pod and place different objects inside. Children can take turns to enter and see what they can see when there is little or no light. Are shiny objects still shiny? Can they make out any colours?

Testing sunglasses

The children could investigate a selection of sunglasses to find out which are the best for blocking light. They could use a light sensor attached to a data logger to take measurements of how much light passes through each pair of sunglasses. They could then devise their own ranking system and present the findings.

Musical toys

Investigate unusual ways to make sounds such as Boomwhackers, giggle tubes and plastic whirly tubes (corrugaphone). Describe how they make sounds. How could they make louder or quieter, or change the pitch?

Staying safe

There are a couple of important safety points to consider before carrying out investigations involving light. The children should be warned that very bright lights can seriously damage their vision. Make them aware that they should never look directly at the Sun, even when wearing sunglasses.

Cross-curricular links and opportunities

Light

Children could look at stained-glass windows and make their own out of different coloured cellophane, or they could design them on the computer and print on to acetate sheets. They could look at festivals like Diwali, Christmas and Hanukkah, and how lights and candles are important. They could make Chinese lanterns and candle holders.

The children could look at how light and shadow is used in art. They could experiment with colour mixing and learn how mixing paint is different from mixing light. Overlaying coloured acetates on an overhead projector is a good way of demonstrating colour mixing. The children could use painting computer programs to explore how changing the red, green and blue values produces different colours, and connect this to an investigation into how colour television pictures are created.

The children could use mirrors to draw self-portraits or try mirror writing. They could look at different optical illusions by artists such as M.C. Escher and Salvador Dali and use these as inspiration to create their own illusions.

Sound

There are clear links with this topic area to the teaching of music. Children can investigate different musical instruments and the different ways that they produce sounds. They could sort instruments into those you pluck, those you bang and those you blow. They can explore how to make the sounds louder and how to change the pitch.

This could also link to Art and Design, with the children using junk materials to create their own musical instruments or different types of hanging wind chimes.

In literacy, children could be introduced to poems related to sound such as 'The Sound Collector' by Roger McGough. The children could then write their own versions.

Progression

Properties of materials can be explored in Year 1. Later, children look at light and how we see things. They think about how light can be reflected and explore how to make shadows. They then look at sounds and compare how light and sound travel. They can use their knowledge of light in the Earth and Space unit, looking at how we get day and night and see the Moon. Finally, they consider how light travels in straight lines and how this can be used to explain why we get shadows.

Suggested scientists

Many scientists are involved in light and sound who could be featured here that children might like to research. Some examples include:

- **Patricia Bath** Ophthalmologist and inventor, she is renowned for her innovative contributions to saving sight through the development of the laserphaco probe for cataract treatment.
- **Hedy Lamarr** Actress and inventor, co-patented a ground-breaking system that contributed to the development of modern Wi-Fi technology.
- **Percy Shaw** Inventor of the cat's eye used in roads all over the world.
- **William Derham** English scientist and clergyman. The first person to accurately measure the speed of sound.

Further reading and resources

Make a straw flute: www.fizzicseducation.com.au/150-science-experiments/light-sound-experiments/make-a-straw-flute/
Marvin and Milo: https://spark.iop.org/collections/marvin-and-milo
Online Tone Generator: www.szynalski.com/tone-generator/
SPACE Project Research Report (1990a): Light: www.stem.org.uk/resources/elibrary/resource/29216/space-project-research-report-light
SPACE Project Research Report (1990b): Sound: www.stem.org.uk/resources/elibrary/resource/29213/space-project-research-report-sound

PART 3

CHAPTER 13

Planning for Good Science

Introduction

Lesson planning is something that many new teachers worry about and struggle with. There is no recipe for the perfect lesson, but successful lessons share many of the same features.

In this chapter we will look at some of the things to consider when planning a science lesson, as well as what to look for when planning a sequence of lessons. We will also look at some of the guidance for putting together a whole science curriculum.

The national curriculum

Always remember to refer back to the national curriculum document when planning. The Notes and Guidance box contains good ideas for things you might like to do in the lesson. The 'pupils might work scientifically' paragraph is always a good place to start for practical ideas for the lesson.

What does good science look like?

Ofsted (2021) identified a number of principles that contribute to high-quality science education:

- Planning the science curriculum so that pupils build knowledge of the key concepts and their relationships over many years. This prevents pupils from seeing science as a list of isolated facts.

- Ensuring that pupils remember the content that has been taught to them over the long term. It states that this is important 'because building domain-specific knowledge leads to expertise'.
- Explicitly teaching pupils the concepts and procedures needed to work scientifically.
- Introducing pupils to a wide-ranging vocabulary.
- Giving clear explanations that build on what pupils already know and explicitly focus pupils' attention on the content being learned.
- Making sure that practical work has a clear purpose and forms part of a wider teaching sequence, only taking place when pupils have enough prior knowledge to learn from the activity.

Components of a science lesson

Clear learning objectives

Learning objectives describe what the pupils should know, understand or be able to do by the end of the lesson. The learning objective is the bedrock of your lesson, on which you can then build your lesson plan.

The learning objectives for a lesson should focus on both knowledge and skills:

- Knowledge outcomes: key science ideas and concepts.
- Skills outcomes: skills related to working scientifically.

Learning objectives put the lesson in context, letting the pupils understand how what they will be doing fits in with the bigger picture. They should be written in a language that is easily understood. Learning objectives can be reviewed during the plenary at the end of the lesson.

Effective learning objectives state what the pupils will learn in the lesson, rather than what they will do. For example: 'To be able to explain how the phases of the Moon are formed' or 'Understand what a plant needs to stay healthy' are good examples of learning objectives.

Objectives could even be written as a 'key learning question', a way of reframing the statement of what pupils will learn with a thought-provoking question, which the teaching and learning in the lesson will address or answer (Durran, 2021).

Ideas for starting the lesson

A good lesson starter should engage and motivate pupils immediately, providing a hook upon which the rest of the lesson hangs. The more engaging the hook, the more motivated the pupils will be during the remainder of the lesson. This might include:

- **Mystery object** Show the pupils an object related to the lesson and ask them to come up with questions about it.
- **Images** Display an image that will make the pupils think. You could zoom in or hide most of the image and ask the pupils to guess what they think it is.
- **Odd one out** Present the pupils with words, phrases or images, and ask them to identify the odd one out, justifying their answers.
- **Video** Show a short video clip to introduce the lesson topic. Pose an interesting question about the video and ask the pupils to work in pairs to try to answer it.
- **Retrieval task** A low-stakes strategy to recall information from a previous lesson. This could take the form of a quick quiz, a brain dump or drawing a quick concept map.

Websites such as Explorify provide useful resources that can be great as a lesson starter to provoke questions, recall and discussions.

Retrieval practice

Retrieval practice describes the process of recalling information from memory with little or minimal prompting. Low-stakes tests (such as individual questions or quizzes) are often used as methods of retrieval practice as these require pupils to think hard about what information they have retained and can recall (EEF, 2021).

This often takes the form of low-stakes quizzing, which could include many different forms, such as:

- multiple-choice questions;
- short-answer fact questions;
- short problem-solving;
- labelling diagrams;
- recitation of quotes or definitions;
- list creation.

(From EEF, 2021)

Retrieval practice can be used quite effectively as a lesson starter, but it shouldn't just be restricted to the start of the lesson (Jones, 2022). For a more detailed guide to retrieval practice, an essential read is Kate Jones's book *Retrieval Practice: Primary*, which I highly recommend.

Practical work

The purpose of any practical work should be clearly defined (Ofsted, 2021). Is the practical work designed to support the learning of an aspect of knowledge, or is carrying it out a goal in itself? It might be that the practical activity itself is the goal, such as helping the pupils to learn how to use a thermometer or carry out another aspect of scientific enquiry.

Ofsted (2021, 2023) suggests that high-quality practical work has a clear purpose, forms part of a wider instructional sequence and takes place only when pupils have enough prior knowledge to learn from the activity.

When planning for a science practical, consider:

- What is the learning objective?
- What could be your starting point?
- What questions could you ask?
- What do you want the children to do?
- How will they record what they do?
- What are the possible outcomes?

Risk assessment

If you are including any practical work or a demonstration, then a risk assessment is essential, even if the assessment is that there is no risk.

Are you using any chemicals that might pose a risk? Consult CLEAPSS as a starting point as well as the ASE book *Be Safe* (2010).

Risk assessment is covered in more detail in Chapter 18.

Progression of science ideas and content

In their research review of science (2021), Ofsted describes a high-quality science curriculum as something that plans for how pupils will build knowledge over time.

Early science draws on pupils' experiences of the world around them, such as local plants, their pets, their own bodies, shadows, etc. Simple explanations can be given for some phenomena, which are then revisited as the pupils get older.

Progression of scientific ideas

In their book *The Teaching of Science in Primary Schools*, Harlen and Qualter (2018) outlined several different dimensions to the progression of ideas. These are:

- From a description to an explanation. Younger pupils may be able to describe a phenomenon. Older pupils will be able to offer more of an explanation.
- From small to big ideas. Small ideas allow the pupils to make sense of specific situations and become bigger as they are linked together into general principles that can be applied to other situations.
- From personal to shared ideas. Young pupils look at things from their own point of view and interpret them based on this thinking. As they develop, their ideas are influenced by those of others.

Cognitive theory and primary science teaching

Cognitive science is gaining increasing influence in education, and many existing and developing educational approaches are described as 'inspired by cognitive science' (EEF, 2021).

One of the main cognitive science concepts that concerns teachers is the processes that we use to create memories. Memory can be separated into sensory, working and long-term, and the relationship between these types of memory can have an impact on how we learn.

The key principles behind this are:

1. Learning requires information to be committed to long-term memory.
2. Information is processed through the working memory.
3. The working memory has limited capacity and can be overloaded.

Teaching/learning approaches supported by cognitive psychology to include in your primary science curriculum are:

- **Reducing cognitive load** The amount of information our working memory can hold at any one time.
- **Retrieval practice** Using a variety of low-stakes strategies to recall information from memory – for example, flashcards, quizzes or mind-mapping.
- **Spaced practice** Distributing learning and retrieval opportunities over a longer period of time rather than concentrating them in 'massed' practice.
- **Interleaving** Sequencing learning tasks so that similar items are interspersed with slightly (but not completely) different types of items rather than being presented consecutively.
- **Dual coding** Using both verbal and non-verbal information (such as words and pictures) alongside each other to teach concepts.

For comprehensive guides to the evidence that underpins these cognitive science approaches, read the Education Endowment Foundation (2021) review as well as McMahon et al. (2021). For dual coding, read Caviglioli (2019).

Structuring a lesson to reduce cognitive load

Cognitive load theory is based on the premise that before entering long-term memory and forming 'schemas' (knowledge structures, such as science concepts or skills) information from the senses must first be processed in a kind of mental holding space known as the 'working memory' (McMahon et al., 2021).

To manage cognitive load, you might use a lesson structure that breaks up complex content into more manageable chunks, such as this from Wardell (2022):

- **Do now** Children complete a retrieval practice activity that encourages them to recall and elaborate on prior knowledge.
- **New learning** Introduce key scientific vocabulary and the new idea/concept.
- **Talk task/let's explore** Use the new scientific language verbally with partners or groups or explore the new key concept in a physical way.
- **Develop learning** Provide additional information that deepens their understanding of the new vocabulary or key concept that is being taught.
- **Independent task** A task that allows them to apply the new concept.
- **Consolidation** Answer a key question that allows them to deepen their new knowledge.

Other strategies to reduce cognitive load

In practice, 'reducing cognitive load' means structuring the knowledge and teaching into smaller chunks to prevent overloading the brain. The pace of the teaching is such that children have a secure set of ideas before they are expected to use them independently (McMahon et al., 2021).

This can include:

- Use focused assessment to elicit pupils' current conceptual ideas, skills and knowledge.
- Present new material in steps.
- Use worked examples – for example, first make classification keys with sweets or finger puppets before applying it to animals or plants.
- Scaffold children's enquiries with planning boards and gradually handover responsibility for making the decisions to pupils.
- Focus teaching on one aspect of Working Scientifically during an investigation. Consider which choices are for children to make.
- Limit what has to be recorded: use focused recording – for example, drawings, written responses to specific questions, instead of lengthy 'write-ups'.

(From McMahon et al., 2021)

Further reading and resources

Lockyer, S. (2016) *Lesson Planning for Primary School Teachers*. London: Bloomsbury.

Nicholson, D. (2021) Primary Science Curriculum Route Map: www.sciencefix.co.uk/2021/01/primary-science-curriculum-route-map/

PLAN: Planning for assessment: PLAN Knowledge matrices: www.planassessment.com/plan-knowledge-matrices-teacher

Shibli, D. (2021) 'How to plan a brilliant lesson': https://edu.rsc.org/ideas/how-to-plan-a-brilliant-lesson-as-a-trainee-teacher/4013898.article

CHAPTER 14

Assessment, Questioning and Pupil Talk

Introduction

Assessment is at the heart of teaching and learning. It allows teachers to make informed decisions about the needs of our learners in order to make further progress. Why do teachers need to assess? The main reasons for assessment are:

- To inform pupils about their own learning and progress.
- To inform the school about the pupils' learning, progress and attainment.
- To inform parents about their children's learning and progress.
- To inform planning for future teaching.

There are two main types of assessment: formative and summative.

Formative assessment Runs alongside the learning and informs the teacher and the children about next steps: Assessment **for** Learning.

Summative assessment Takes place at the end of a block of learning and sums up where learners have reached in relation to agreed benchmarks. Usually this takes the form of an end- of-unit quiz or test: Assessment **of** Learning.

Formative assessment

Formative assessment, sometimes called Assessment for Learning (AFL), runs alongside the learning and informs the teacher and the children about next steps. It is ongoing and a regular part of the teacher's role. Formative assessment is an essential component of classroom work and its development can raise standards of achievement (Black and William, 2010).

Leahy et al. (2005) identified five teaching strategies that are common in effective formative assessment:

- Clarifying learning intentions and criteria for success.
- Engineering effective classroom discussions and other learning tasks that elicit evidence of student understanding.
- Providing feedback that moves learners forward.
- Activating students as instructional resources for one another.
- Activating students as the owners of their own learning.

Formative assessment allows teachers to determine their children's needs and their current level of understanding. This can allow teachers to make an informed choice. It might inform future planning, giving teachers a guide for how to adapt the next activity to build on a learner's current understanding or skills level.

The climate in the classroom is very important. AFL will flourish best when children feel confident and safe in the classroom and when they feel comfortable about sharing their ideas without ridicule or embarrassment (Hodgson, 2010).

Assessment as learning

Assessment as learning draws on the cognitive principle that children are more likely to remember knowledge if they practise retrieving that knowledge over extended periods of time. It involves children recalling information successfully from long-term memory into their working memory (Ofsted, 2021).

Retrieval practice refers to the act of recalling learned information from memory, and in doing so the memory is made stronger (Jones, 2019). Younger children benefit from a more guided retrieval practice task – for example, adding knowledge to a partially completed concept map (Ofsted, 2021).

There is more on retrieval practice as a strategy in Chapter 13.

Questioning in primary science

Questioning is an integral part of the teaching process, particularly in science. It is said that teachers ask nearly 400 questions a day. Questioning enables teachers to check children's understanding at key points in the lesson. It also encourages engagement and focuses the children's thinking on key concepts and ideas (Chin, 2007).

Teachers can use questions in different ways:

- Questions for finding out children's ideas: 'What do you think is happening . . . ?'
- Questions for encouraging predictions: 'What do you think will happen if . . . ?'
- Questions to encourage planning: 'How will you make this a fair test?'
- Questions to encourage further questions: 'What other things would you like to know about rainforests?'

Open and closed questions

Closed questions are often used to evaluate what children know. The teacher asks a closed question that is basically information-seeking, that requires a predetermined short answer, and that is usually pitched at the recall or lower-order cognitive level (Chin, 2007).

Closed questions can be answered with either a short word or phrase, or a simple yes or no.

Examples of closed questions:

- Is ice a solid?
- Did the cress seeds germinate when water was added?
- Which parachute fell the slowest – the large one or the small one?

In comparison, **open questions** allow the children to give a long answer. They give the children a chance to think and reflect (Chin, 2007). Open questions begin with words such as what, how, why, describe, predict. They can allow for higher order thinking.

Examples of open questions:

- What properties does ice have that made you classify it as a solid?
- Describe what conditions are needed for cress seeds to germinate?
- How did the size of the parachute affect the speed at which it falls?

Bloom's Taxonomy and questioning

Questioning enables teachers to check children's understanding at key points in the lesson. It also encourages engagement and focuses their thinking on key concepts and ideas.

Bloom's Taxonomy (1956) is a classification system that can be used to help plan and formulate higher order questions. It arranges questions based on their level of complexity, from basic knowledge and understanding of a concept or process to higher levels of critical and creative thinking.

Table 14.1   Using Bloom's Taxonomy: some possible question stems

Level	Question stems
Knowledge (Basic recall)	What, when, who, how, identify. What is . . . ? Who was it that . . . ? Can you name . . . ? What happened after . . . ? Which one . . . ? Where is . . . ?
Comprehension (Demonstrating understanding)	Compare, predict, explain, contrast. Can you explain why . . . ? Can you clarify . . . ? Can you write an outline of . . . ? What was the main idea . . . ? How would you summarise . . . ? How are these things similar/different . . . ?
Application (Using knowledge)	Build, plan, how would, test. Could you give another instance when . . . ? What other ways could we plan this . . . ? What does the graph tell us about . . . ? What questions would you ask about . . . ? How will you find out X . . . ?
Analysis (Examining information)	Why did this happen . . . ? What would have happened if . . . ? How is X related to Y? What evidence can you find to . . . ? What conclusions can you make . . . ? What was the problem with . . . ?
Synthesis (Creating something new)	Could you design . . . ? How might you stop X happening . . . ? What would happen if . . . ? Would this happen if we changed . . . ? How would you test . . . ? Can you predict the result if . . . ?
Evaluation (Assessing value)	Is there a better way to do . . . ? Is this a good or bad thing . . . ? How good were your results . . . ? What information would you use to support the view . . . ?

Questioning techniques

Some different questioning techniques to try include:

- **Turn to your neighbour** Children discuss the question with someone sitting nearby.

- **Think-pair-share** Children first think individually, then discuss with a partner and then share their thinking with the class.
- **Cold calling** The teacher asks the question and then chooses a child to answer without raising their hands. Ask the question first before naming a student. If you use a pupil name first, the rest of the class will switch off and not listen to the question.
- **Mini whiteboards** All children use individual whiteboards to write down their answer and then hold them up to show the teacher.
- **Bounce it** The teacher chooses a child to answer, but if that child doesn't know the answer, they can choose to 'bounce' it to another child. That child explains it to them, and the original child then tells the teacher the answer.
- **Agree, build, challenge** Or ABC questioning. Once a child answers the question, another child can say whether they agree and why. A different child can be chosen to build upon this answer, and another could challenge it and suggest a different answer.

Using mini whiteboards

When used properly, mini whiteboards are an excellent resource which, once children are shown the best way to use them, can make a real difference to whole-class assessment.

Rosenshine's *Principles of Instruction* (2012) says that effective teachers will fre-quently check to see that all children are learning the material being introduced to them. Mini whiteboards allow the teacher to stop and gauge whether the class understand something. They can give a very quick snapshot of the whole class. They allow for quick identification of misconceptions that the children might have that can then be challenged or corrected.

Ask a question. Give time for the children to write their answers on the boards, then ask them all to hold them up and show you. Use an agreed command such as '3-2-1 Show me'.

Support with assessment

Teacher Assessment in Primary Science TAPS is an excellent bank of resources to support teachers and schools in developing their assessment systems. It's an excellent resource for all primary teachers to investigate..

PLAN assessment PLAN includes knowledge matrices, vocabulary lists and progression guides to help teachers understand the science content they are teaching and how it links to other years. There are also examples of pupil work which can be used for moderation.

Encouraging talk in the primary classroom

Pupil talk provides them with a way to develop and express their ideas, as well as comparing them with the ideas of others, which helps to develop critical thinking.

Right across the curriculum, talk engages children, motivates them to use their speaking and listening skills, and helps them learn how to respect and respond to each other (RSC, 2015).

Pupil-to-pupil talk

Talking in science helps pupils to make sense of what we want them to learn. It helps them to develop an ability to reason scientifically.

In successful pupil-to-pupil discussion, all members of a group contribute, and all opinions and ideas are respected.

Pupil-to-teacher talk

The ways that teachers talk to pupils can take different forms at different parts of the lesson. Research found that science teachers needed to use different kinds of talk to enable children to move from their existing everyday understanding of natural phenomena towards a scientific view (CUREE, 2011). These included 'dialogic' episodes when teachers probed pupils' everyday ideas and 'authoritative' episodes when the teacher introduced scientific ideas.

Dialogic talk involves exploring answers from children by asking for more detail or asking others in the class whether they agree or disagree.

Authoritative talk is where teachers keep the focus on the science points being addressed rather than addressing the children's own ideas.

Examples of dialogic talk:

- That's interesting – what do you mean by that?
- Do you agree with what Amy has just said?
- Could you explain more about what you just said?

Questions are important within science lessons. Diagnostic questions can be used to help the teacher monitor levels of understanding and to identify possible misconceptions.

Strategies for encouraging talk

Children are rarely offered guidance or training in how to communicate effectively in groups (Mercer et al., 2009) and many children rarely encounter examples of such discussion in their lives outside school. Introduce regular opportunities for the children to become used to talking about science and exploring their thinking.
There are many different strategies you could use, such as:

Odd one out The class is shown three or four different pictures (or real objects) and asked to say which is the odd one out and why. The 'why' is key – the children justify their reasoning and so reveal their thinking. There's usually no single correct answer. Any one of the options could be chosen, as long as the reasoning is valid – for example, an image of a bar of chocolate, a bottle of water and a balloon.

PMI (plus, minus, interesting) The class is given a scenario or a statement and then asked to consider the positives, the minuses and any interesting associated ideas. For example, what if nothing decayed? What if all sounds had the same pitch?

Big questions Give the class a chance to discuss something big. Prompt with a picture, an object or a simple demonstration of a process to engage them and to support your question. Why don't birds get electrocuted on power lines? Do aliens exist?, etc.

Concept cartoons These can be used as a means of stimulating small group discussion. The children can discuss the scenario and then give their own explanations. These are very useful for introducing a working scientifically activity.

Talking points These are statements about a topic that can be either factually accurate, open to debate or simply wrong. Children decide in pairs whether the statements are true or false.

Using images A powerful image can be a good stimulus to encourage children to engage in effective talk in science. They can also be used as a starting point for enquiry.

Support for pupil talk

The Primary Science Teaching Trust (PSTT) has some excellent resources for encouraging Pupil Talk in Science as part of what they call 'Bright Ideas Time'. They also have an excellent Pictures for Talk resource from the PSTT with some useful images and questions to get you started.

Explorify is a good free source of odd-one-out activities, PMI situations and big questions you could use.

BEST Evidence Science Teaching is a collection of free diagnostic questions to reveal children's misconceptions with response activities to help the teacher challenge misconceptions and develop understanding.

Further reading and resources

BEST Evidence Science Teaching (7–11): www.stem.org.uk/primary/resources/collections/science/best-evidence-science-teaching

Bright Ideas Time: https://pstt.org.uk/resources/curriculum-materials/bright-ideas

Centre for Industry Education Collaboration (CIEC): Enabling Accurate Teacher Assessment in Primary Science: www.york.ac.uk/ciec/resources/primary/enabling-accurate-teacher-assessment/

Pictures for Talk: https://pstt.org.uk/resources/curriculum-materials/Pictures-for-Talk

PLAN: Planning for assessment: www.planassessment.com/

Teacher Assessment in Primary Science (TAPS): https://pstt.org.uk/unique-resources/taps/

Teacherhead: https://teacherhead.com/2012/08/28/the-number-1-bit-of-classroom-kit-mini-whiteboards/

CHAPTER 15

Taking Science Outside

Introduction

Only around 8 per cent of school-age children in England get out of their classrooms into green spaces (Natural Connections, 2016) during school time. Taking science outside of the primary classroom can provide first-hand experiences of the local environment that allow pupils to observe science taking place in the real world. This embeds their learning of science into meaningful contexts and provides opportunities for novel and exciting learning experiences.

All schools will have some outdoor space that they can use. Even inner-city schools with no green spaces can still take science outside into the playground (Natural Connections, 2016).

Benefits of outdoor learning

There is a substantial body of evidence that shows a positive link between learning in the natural environments and a very wide range of learning processes and outcomes, and health and well-being outcomes too (Dillon and Lovell, 2022).

In a study by Natural Connections (2016), 92 per cent of teachers said that pupils were more engaged with learning when outdoors and 85 per cent saw a positive impact on their behaviour. Of the staff surveyed, 90 per cent found outdoor learning to be useful for curriculum delivery.

Malone (2008) found that children engaged in learning outside the classroom:

- attain higher levels of knowledge and skills;
- improve their physical health and increase their motor skills;

- socialise and interact in new and different ways with their peers and adults;
- show improved attention, enhanced self-concept, self-esteem and mental health;
- change their environmental behaviours and their values and attitudes.

An Ofsted (2008) study showed that first-hand experiences of learning outside the classroom help to make subjects more vivid and interesting for pupils and also enhance their understanding.

Taking science outside plays a role in connecting the school to the neighbourhood and the world at large (Dillon et al., 2005). Spending more time outside the classroom helps to develop a greater understanding and love for the environment. Outdoor and environmental education weaves an important thread through the teaching of sustainability and climate change (Hoath and Dave, 2022).

Planning to go outside

When planning to take the pupils outside, consider:

- What are the learning objectives and benefits? Be clear about why learning is taking place in a particular environment (Spring, 2021). What do you want the pupils to experience and what skills do you want them to acquire?
- How many additional staff and helpers will you need? Keep them informed of the learning objectives and how they will support the pupils.
- What are the potential risks? How will you minimise them? Carry out a risk assessment before you go.

For more on risk assessment, see Chapter 18.

- How will you help the pupils to understand how the outdoor experiences connect to the work carried out in the classroom?
- What in-class activities will you carry out to follow up on the outdoor activities?
- Where can you go for more help and support? There are many outdoor learning and field studies websites that provide information and advice, some of which you will find in the further reading and resources section at the end of this chapter.
- If you're going to an external venue such as a zoo, they will usually be able to provide guidance on planning a safe and fun experience, so do ask them if they have any teacher guides or planning checklists you can use.

Science whatever the weather

Learning in the 'outdoor classroom' should take place regularly throughout the year. Going outdoors should not be reserved for the occasional school trip, but should be a normal part of the school day throughout the year (Forsey, 2014).

Outdoor science can take place whatever the weather, and in some cases it is the weather that provides the science. Be sure to dress appropriately with waterproof clothes, gloves and wellies if necessary (Forsey, 2014).

Handy equipment

The exact equipment you need will depend on the nature of the activity, but there are some items that will always prove useful. These include:

- Clipboards, paper and pens.
- Hand lenses or magnifying glasses.
- Plastic pots with lids and clear plastic bags for collecting specimens.
- Tape measures and rulers.
- White trays for collecting samples.
- String for marking out areas.
- Small quadrants for sampling (wire coat-hangers pulled out into a square or squares made from sticks tied together with rubber bands).
- A digital camera or tablet computer for taking photographs.
- Cleansing wipes and hand sanitiser gel.

To help the children (and teachers!) identify any plants and animals they might find when investigating living things outside the classroom, it helps to have some identification guides handy.

Consider making up some outdoor learning kits in large plastic boxes with secure lids. Have them ready to go outside (or even keep them outside).

Assign children to be outdoor monitors and to take responsibility for putting the boxes out in the morning and bringing them in at the end of the day.

Setting up a space for outdoor learning does not have to be expensive. Nicky Bolton (2020) describes setting up a 'Bucket School', where 30 upturned buckets provide the seating for a class outside, as well as a container to collect samples in. Strong builders' buckets are recommended.

Using the school grounds

Ofsted (2013) describes how good schools had embraced outdoor learning and used their outdoor learning areas to teach environmental science, allowing their pupils to experience science in action, regularly and at first hand. The areas around the school provide a rich, easy- to-access, learning resource.

Consider the facilities available to you at your school. Is there a school nature area or school garden that can be used? Does the school have a pond?

If the school does not have a nature area or garden, could a class project be to set one up? Perhaps the pupils could design a place for insects to live in or a small flowerbed to attract pollinating insects like bees and butterflies.

Taking messy things outside

Sometimes, going outside makes certain activities easier to deal with, especially if there is a risk of mess. This includes:

- planting bulbs and seeds;
- activities using water such as floating and sinking;
- elephant's toothpaste or coke and mentos;
- looking at how a drum skin vibrates by putting bird seed on it, then hitting it with a drumstick. Leave the seed for the birds to eat when you're done!

Opportunities for taking science outside

There are many different activities that we do as part of the science curriculum which can work very well when taken outside. Some of them are listed below.

Outdoor biology

The various biology units provide some of the most obvious opportunities for going outside. If you intend to ask the children to think about living things, habitats and the environment, then it makes sense to get outside and see them for real.

Activities include seasonal changes. Look at the changes in trees and plants over the course of a school year. Take photographs and/or record short videos of the green areas of the school. This can all be collated and compared in the summer term.

Studying plants

- Looking at flowers: parts of a flower; wind vs. insect pollinated.
- Looking at leaves: comparing, classifying.
- Classifying the trees around the school: from leaves/fruits; make a map.
- Height of trees around the school.
- Bark rubbings.

Exploring habitats

- Collecting minibeasts.
- Measuring conditions in different habitats/microhabitats – light level, temperature, etc.
- Looking where different plants grow.
- Life in a tree: hold a sheet under a low branch and shake the branch – see what minibeasts fall out.

Sampling and surveys

- Coat-hanger quadrants: stretch wire coat hanger into a square and study the plants inside the area.
- String safari: study plants along 1m of string laid across the field.
- Which colour flowers do insects like best?
- Comparing plants in different areas – light/shade.
- Camouflage: drop coloured spaghetti into grass to see which is easiest to spot.

Growing plants and gardening

- Build raised beds/square foot gardening.
- Grow bulbs and seeds outside.
- Grow your own potatoes.

Large area needed

- Looking at how heart rate changes with exercise.
- Modelling circulation (need a large area to move around).

OPAL surveys

The Opal Programme provides resources for carrying out citizen science surveys of the natural environment around the UK. This includes topics such as soil and earthworms, minibeasts, biodiversity, tree health, and more. The surveys are closed for data entry, but you can still access the resources and run them as a class project.

Outdoor chemistry

For chemistry/materials activities, the main reason for going outside is usually because it's going to get messy.

- Diet Coke and Mentos.
- Exploring bubbles and bubble mixtures.
- Alka-Seltzer rockets.
- Elephant's toothpaste.
- Bicarb and vinegar.

However, being outside might form part of the activity, such as:

- Materials walks.
- Evaporation of puddles.
- Drying clothes, comparing inside to outside.

Outdoor physics

Where the outside is important

Sound trails Walk around the school grounds and listen at various points along the route to see what sounds can be heard (Grimshaw et al., 2019).

Playground physics Look at different outdoor playground equipment. How do they work? What forces are involved?

Exploring shadows Look at how the shadows move through the course of a day.

Making sundials Make a sundial (plenty of templates online) and test it out in the playground. Would your school consider getting a sundial printed onto your playground which could be used at any time by the children?

Where you need a lot of space

- Mapping out the scale of the solar system.
- Modelling how the Sun, Earth and Moon move.
- Making string telephones.
- Making water rockets.
- Exploring parachutes and helicopters.
- Air resistance: running with umbrellas open vs. closed.
- Making catapults.
- Investigating the speed of sound.
- Investigating whether sound travels in all directions.
- Making paper aeroplanes.

Where it might get wet/messy

- Sailing boats in guttering filled with water.
- Water resistance: dropping plasticine shapes into measuring cylinders.
- Floating and sinking with bowls of water.
- Explore vibrations with drums and bird seed.
- Movement of cars on different surfaces, tarmac, grass, mud, gravel, etc.

Taking technology outside

The outdoor classroom can definitely benefit from the addition of mobile technology. Digital cameras are great for recording images of samples that you find and can be used in video mode to record sounds as well as video. Of course, tablets can do all of this as well if you have them. Digital microscopes can be attached to a class laptop to view samples of leaves and materials close up.

Many data-logging interfaces are portable and as such can be used outside. The temperature and light probes can be used to take the temperature of ponds and the light level beneath a tree canopy, for example.

For more on data logging, see Chapter 16.

If you haven't got tablets, then stand-alone digital thermometers, light-level meters and sound-level meters can also be used.

For identification of plants that you find outside, there are a selection of tablet apps you can use, such as:

- ID apps such as Plant Net (free).
- Google lens (free).
- LeafSnap tree and shrub identification.
- Picture This.
- iNaturalist app.

School nature areas

Nature areas can be an oasis for wildlife in urban areas. Even if your school is in a leafy suburb, many gardens are over-managed and not very friendly to birds and wildlife. Nature areas can provide a safe and attractive place for the children to learn about wildlife.

A nature area provides children with science on their doorstep. There is a lot of science involved in planning and setting up a nature area. The children can research the places where insects like to live, or the types of plant that attract bees and other pollinators. A nature area allows the teaching of the life cycles of insects and plants since the children have easy access to observe insects and flowers in the wild. A school pond might also provide tadpoles.

By building a nature area, children can be encouraged to think about their local environment and how it can be made more attractive to wildlife and to people. Setting up a school nature area can be an exciting project that can benefit the school as well as local wildlife. This doesn't have to be a major construction project, and a few simple ideas can still provide good learning opportunities.

There are many different activities that the children can do, such as setting up a bug hotel, a compost area, wildflower gardens for pollinators and bird/insect feeders. You might even try to build a school pond.

There are many guides on how to build these on websites like The Wildlife Trust, RSPB or Royal Horticultural Society.

Are there any charities that can help? Some woodland charities provide saplings to schools. Speak to your local garden centre or builders' merchants to see if they are willing to donate any spare plants or building materials. You might be able to involve the local community in fundraising and offering help for the heavier jobs.

Further reading and resources

Barnett, J. and Feasey, R. (2016) *Jumpstart! Science Outdoors: Cross-curricular Games and Activities for Ages 5–12*. Oxford: Routledge.

Council for Learning Outside the Classroom (CLOtC): www.lotc.org.uk/

Grow Your Own Potatoes (GYOP): www.growyourownpotatoes.org.uk/

Grow Your Own Salad: www.foodgrowingschools.org/

Learning through Landscapes: https://ltl.org.uk/

OPAL Citizen Science Surveys: www.imperial.ac.uk/opal/surveys/

Outdoor Classroom Day: https://outdoorclassroomday.com/

RHS Campaign for School Gardening: https://schoolgardening.rhs.org.uk/Resources/

Science Fix: Teaching Primary Science Outside of the Classroom: www.sciencefix.co.uk/2020/06/teaching-primary-science-outside-of-the-classroom/

Science and Plants for Schools: Beyond the Classroom: www.saps.org.uk/resource-collections/beyond-the-classroom/

Square Foot Gardening: https://squarefootgardening.org

Tree Tools for Schools: www.treetoolsforschools.org.uk/

The Wildlife Trusts: Guides for building bug hotels, wildlife ponds and more: www.wildlifetrusts.org/actions

The Woodland Trust Outdoor Learning Pack: www.woodlandtrust.org.uk/media/43645/outdoor-learning-resource-pack.pdf

CHAPTER 16

Science and Computing/ICT

Introduction

Information and Communication Technology (ICT) has become such an important part of our everyday lives. It's hard to imagine a world without the internet and its wealth of online resources to support teaching and learning. Until quite recently, the technology available in schools was limited to desktop and laptop computers. Nowadays, you're also likely to have access to visualisers, interactive whiteboards, digital cameras and maybe tablets/iPads if the school budget allows.

The pandemic made us all much more aware of the range of collaboration tools such as Zoom, Teams, Google Workspace and Office 365, and how they enable us to communicate and work collaboratively with teachers and students around the world.

Technology alone does not make a difference to learning. Rather, how well the technology is used to support teaching and learning is the key determinant of its impact (Higgins et al., 2012). Technology should be used in the classroom when it is appropriate, not just for the sake of it, and it should enhance the teaching of science in the lesson rather than being a distraction.

This is always such a difficult subject to write about, as technology changes fast and any websites and apps that I recommend may suddenly vanish or stop working. Developments such as Artificial Intelligence (AI) are in their infancy right now and are only going to become more ingrained into everything we do as teachers over the coming years. For up-to-date information on the use of ICT in general and within science, visit my two blogs: www.whiteboardblog.co.uk and www.sciencefix.co.uk.

Creative computing in the national curriculum

While the focus of the changes to the national curriculum for computing (DfE, 2013b) was on the introduction of coding and programming, it still states that pupils should be taught the following:

In KS1: use technology purposefully to create, organise, store, manipulate and retrieve digital content.

In KS2: select, use and combine a variety of software (including internet services) on a range of digital devices to design and create a range of programs, systems and content that accomplish given goals, including collecting, analysing, evaluating and presenting data and information.

These statements cover a wide variety of activities, creatively using different digital tools and platforms and creating a broad range of media including text, images, sound, animations and video. Ensure that your pupils experience working across this full range. This can include Microsoft Office and Google Workspace software, but also video editing, sound recording, animation creation and other software. There are plenty of opportunities in science to do this, as well as across the whole primary curriculum.

Presenting science using ICT ('digital storytelling')

Put simply, 'digital storytelling' is the use of computer-based tools to present information. There are many different ways to do this, from making movies, recording voices, creating animations or writing electronic books.

In science, technology can help to take a mundane task – such as writing a report, explaining a process or describing an experiment – and allow the pupils to demonstrate their understanding in more creative ways.

Can the children use technology to do more than 'go and write it up'? Can they tell a story about their experiment and what they found out? It's not something that you will do every lesson, but from time to time where the curriculum allows. There are also opportunities for cross-curricular links with computing; could time in a computing lesson be used to produce something linked to a recent science lesson?

For example, pupils can create:

- comic strips;
- e-books;

- photo slideshows;
- slide presentations;
- flyers and information leaflets;
- stop-motion animations;
- short films;
- podcasts and audio recordings.

Churchill and Barratt-Pugh (2020) identified some ways in which digital storytelling supports digital literacy learning in primary schools. These include:

- Engagement: digital storytelling activities provide opportunities for student-centred practices and student engagement.
- Meaningful context: these activities can help students build a greater understanding of the content and skills developed by engaging with the tasks.
- Structure to work with media: these activities provide opportunities to work with multiple forms of digital media.
- Work with technology tools: provides opportunities to use a range of technology tools to plan, produce, present and review their story.
- Research skills: provides opportunities to use carry out guided internet research, and find and process information found online.

Images, audio and video

Digital cameras are now relatively inexpensive and simple to use, and tablets such as iPads also have the ability to record video and audio. Audio recordings can also be made easily on a laptop using software such as Audacity or GarageBand and a cheap microphone.

Pupils can take photographs of things they are studying such as a flower or a pulley and then annotate them using apps such as PicCollage.

Pupils can record videos of practical work and provide a commentary as they go along. Playing back videos allows the pupils to review and evaluate their work. Audio and video files can be shared on the school website or social media channels (if parent permission has been given).

These types of activity can be a great way to include cross-curricular links and allow the pupils to develop their communication, collaboration and literacy skills.

They will need to work together to create scripts, record each other and edit a finished product.

Ideas for audio or video recording include:

- Role-play an interview with a famous scientist like Mary Anning or Charles Darwin.
- Make a news report on a science investigation, explaining the results.
- Record your own version of a gardening show, explaining how to care for plants or how to take a plant cutting.
- Use a green screen to appear in different habitats or microhabitats, and describe the animals and plants you might find living there.
- Produce a radio commercial to advertise a new pet food.
- Promote issues like healthy eating or recycling using public information films.
- Read out science poems or stories written in class, perhaps adding sound effects.

Apps like ChatterPix or websites like Blabberize let you take an image or photograph and make it speak by recording your own audio on top of it. The children could create a talking avatar of a scientist such as Charles Darwin and have him talk about his life and the theory of evolution.

Remember, the technology should be used in the classroom when it is appropriate, not just for the sake of it. It should enhance the teaching of science in the lesson, rather than being a distraction. The teacher should decide when, and when not, to use the technology.

eBooks, comic strips and presentations

Children can create eBooks using tools such as Book Creator and Storybird. An eBook can contain photographs, text, drawings and even audio. The finished books can be read online and shared with parents. eBooks can be used to explain the results of an experiment, demonstrate understanding of a concept or to write a story about the life of a famous scientist.

If you don't have access to tablets, children can use regular presentation software such as PowerPoint or Google Slides to create digital storybooks.

Pupils can also be asked to create comic strips to show what they have learned. In a comic you can't write lots of text, so the children will need to be selective and only include the most important pieces of information. There are some great comic-strip generators available online such as Storyboard That or Canva, or you can download software such as Comic Life.

Figure 16.1   An example comic strip to explain the findings of an investigation

Data handling with technology

Spreadsheets

Technology can support science in schools by helping pupils observe, measure, record, manipulate and interpret results. Data-logging equipment can aid the collection of data, which can then be turned into a graph and/or analysed in a spreadsheet.

Science enquiry practical work can generate plenty of data that can be tabulated, analysed and presented. Software such as data loggers or spreadsheets can be used to quickly create graphs, removing the need to draw them by hand. This can free up more time for analysis. However, such software shouldn't be used every time: it is important that pupils also have the opportunity to practise drawing graphs by hand.

Databases and branching databases

Computer databases can be used to store information. A database consists of 'records' and each record contains 'fields'. These can then be interrogated and graphed. Within science, children can create their own databases, entering data on minibeasts, planets or even themselves (eye colour, hair colour, height, etc.). This data can then be explored and various types of graphs produced to look for patterns.

Branching databases are a special type of database that can be used as a classification key. They can be used when teaching about classifying animals and plants alongside drawing them by hand. This is not something that regular Office software can do and you will need some additional software to do it, such as J2E branch or Purple Mash 2Question.

Data logging

Data logging provides quicker and more accurate data collection, as well as allowing you to monitor changes over long periods of time. To carry out data logging, you need a computer, an interface that communicates with the computer and sensors that communicate with the interface. You will also need special software be able to make sense of the information and display it on the screen.

In the past, to carry out data logging you needed a computer, a data-logging interface that talks to the computer and some sensors that talk to the interface. The computer will also need some special software to be able to make sense of the information it is receiving and display it on the screen. Once you've recorded the data, this can then be downloaded onto a computer for processing, graph drawing, etc. Usually, this can then be exported into software such as Excel. Some data loggers can also connect to iPads and tablets via Bluetooth.

Many different sensors are available: temperature probes are the cheapest and easiest to use. They are therefore the first external sensors you should consider getting. If funds allow, try to get more than one for each data logger, so you can monitor the temperature of two different things at once. Other sensors include motion sensors, timing ramps, light gates, light-level meters, heart-rate monitors, sound-level sensors, and more.

Table 16.1   Suggestions for data-logging activities in the science curriculum. See Nicholson (2019) for the full list

Year	Topic	Experiment	Sensors
3	Forces	How things move on different surfaces.	Timing ramp or light gates
3	Light	Which sunglasses are the best?	Light sensor
4	Living Things and Habitats	Monitor conditions in different habitats over time.	Light, temperature
4	States of Matter	Use different wrappings to see how to keep water cold for the longest (or warm water warm). Which materials are the best insulators?	Temperature
4	Sound	Look at sound insulating materials.	Sound level
4	Sound	Monitor the noise in the classroom/hall/ playground over the course of a day.	Sound level
5	Properties of Materials	Test insulators: which is best for keeping a cup of tea hot the longest?	Temperature
5	Forces	Acceleration due to gravity: speed of a car down a ramp.	Timing ramp, light gates
6	Living Things/ Evolution	Why do some animals have fur? Look at the temperature changes of a plastic cup with no fur and one with fur.	Temperature
6	Living Things/ Evolution	Why do penguins huddle? Look at the temperature changes of a group of cups of hot water vs. one on its own.	Temperature

Note

Phones and tablets can be turned into simple data loggers using apps like Arduino Science Journal or Phyphox. These apps use the microphone and camera as sound/light sensors and can also make use of the motion sensors inside the devices. They can't measure things like temperature. If you've got some old phones lying around, it might be an easier (and cheaper) option to explore data logging.

Simulations

A computer simulation is an on-screen representation of a situation or a process, such as the particles in a material or an electrical circuit. Computer simulations can be a valuable tool for teaching science.

Simulations and models allow pupils to investigate abstract ideas or carry out practical work that would be difficult or time-consuming in the classroom, or that the children would not normally be able to witness – for example, building electric circuits or looking at the motion of the planets (Massie and Long, 2009). A computer simulation enables repeated trials of an experiment to be carried out quickly and easily, and can speed up an experiment to provide immediate feedback (Kara and Yeşilyurt, 2007). They are also very useful for carrying out practical work as part of remote learning.

Always make sure that pupils are supported in their use of simulations. Podolefsky et al. (2010) found that scaffolding is essential to support pupil engagement in science simulations. Ensure that the children are prepared with some level of understanding of the topic or basic vocabulary before embarking on the simulation. Young children in particular will need guidance in their use and a very clear focus.

Examples of simulations

PhET simulations

The PhET site is an excellent resource full of simulations for all ages and subject areas. A great example of these is their DC circuit construction kit. This allows pupils to build and explore electrical circuits. Where possible, allow the pupils to explore a 'real' circuit first, before exploring the simulation.

Unlike in the classroom, there are no limitations on equipment or safety issues, so if the pupils want to know what happens if they use ten batteries, then they can find out!

Solar System Scope

Solar System Scope is a good example of an online orrery, providing a simulation of the motion of the planets around the Sun. You can play the simulation forwards or backwards at different speeds to see how the planets move, or you can drag a specific planet around. You can zoom in on the inner planets or zoom right out to see how the outer planets move.

Scaffold this with a question sheet for the pupils to give them specific things to find out, such as the length of a year on different planets.

Visualisers in primary science

A visualiser (sometimes called a document camera) is essentially a small video camera that produces real-time images on a screen. The camera is typically mounted on an arm pointing downwards. Any object or document placed below the camera is projected up onto the screen for the whole class to see. The visualiser can be connected directly to the screen, or more commonly to the teacher's computer that is itself connected to the screen. Visualisers make it much easier for teachers to show resources and artefacts to the whole class, without having children crowding around struggling to see what is going on (Nicholson, 2011). Using annotation tools, it would then be possible to draw and annotate over the top of the image – perhaps labelling the key features or key words to describe the object.

Ideas for using a visualiser

Ideas for using a visualiser include:

- Looking at flowers. Display a real flower up close and, using the whiteboard tools, pupils could annotate the petal, anther, stigma, sepal and filament.
- Displaying 'minibeasts'. Look closely at invertebrates collected by the pupils from the school grounds such as woodlice, slugs and caterpillars.
- Using the zoom feature to look at objects in high detail such as mouldy bread or different types of fabric. Look closely at natural materials such as wood, rocks, stones, leaves, shells and pine cones.
- Demonstrating how to read scales on rulers, thermometers and other meters.
- Modelling which buttons to use on stopwatches, calculators and data loggers.
- Displaying images from books, photographs, food labels without having to photocopy them.
- Modelling graph drawing with real pencil, ruler and graph paper, rather than trying to use the interactive whiteboard tools.
- Displaying good examples of student work to the whole class.
- Displaying a worksheet – modelling how to fill it in prior to completion during the lesson. Also, for modelling exam questions.

(From Nicholson, 2011)

Digital microscopes

A variation on the visualiser, there are many digital microscopes that are suitable for the primary classroom, such as the TTS Easi-Scope. These allow you to examine objects such as materials and parts of a flower to a higher magnification than would be possible with a normal visualiser. If your budget can stretch to buying one, I highly recommend it.

Virtual field trips

There are many occasions when it would be brilliant to whisk your class away to see the tortoises on the Galapagos Islands or to dive underwater and explore the Great Barrier Reef. Sadly, however, that will not be possible, but using technology you can take them on a virtual field trip, travelling to other countries without actually leaving the classroom. Your classroom screen can become a window on the world, allowing children to view faraway places.

There are many occasions where a trip is not possible – time, cost and safety being the main three – so a virtual trip can at least go some way to letting the children experience what these places look like. A virtual field trip is more than just a slideshow of images. It may include 360° photos and videos that let you move the viewpoint around and look in different directions. They may contain linked images so you feel as if you are moving around the space, and they may also include hotspots – clickable spots that will open up more information as text, audio or video.

Streetview

One of the easiest ways to experience a virtual field trip is with Google Maps and Google Street View. Google has extensively covered most of the world with both satellite imagery and 360° cameras, first on cars and more recently in the backpacks of hikers. Google Street View can give you a sense of standing in the middle of the street, with a full 360° view of the area around you.

If you wanted to take the class on a materials walk and the area around your school isn't the most inspiring, you could go on a trip around a school in a different town or a different country and compare it your own local area.

As well as regular streets, Google has also taken their Street View cameras off-road into places such as the The Eden Project, zoos like London and Chester, and even inside museums like the Science Museum in London.

This could be used instead of a trip, but sometimes it could even be used to prepare for a trip you are going on or to reinforce a trip you have actually been on.

It is also possible to go on curated tours, set up by others. Google Maps Treks lets you explore places such as the Galapagos Islands, the Great Barrier Reef, the Amazon Basin and the Samburu National Reserve in Kenya. Access Mars lets you use actual footage of Mars taken by the Curiosity rover to explore the surface of Mars.

Webcams

There are many websites that allow access to live webcams – for example, sites such as Explore.org and EarthCam. These can let you view live feeds from all over the world. For example, if you were looking at seasonal changes or day and night, you could use a live feed from Australia to show the children that it was nighttime there. There are many nature webcams too – for example, via The Wildlife Trust. In spring-time, children can view nestbox cameras and keep an eye on hatching eggs and (hopefully) developing chicks. Many active volcanoes have webcams too – there's always one erupting somewhere.

Further reading and resources

Access Mars: https://accessmars.withgoogle.com/

Antarctica 360 videos: https://nzaht.org/share/virtual-reality/antarctica-360-vr/

Arduino Science Journal: www.arduino.cc/education/science-journal

Danny's YouTube Channel: www.youtube.com/@DannyNicholsonsTechFix

Earthcam: www.earthcam.com/

Explore.org Nature Cams: https://explore.org/livecams

Google Arts and Culture Places: https://artsandculture.google.com/category/place

Google Earth Tours: www.google.com/earth/about/gallery/

Google Treks: www.google.co.uk/maps/about/treks

Natural History Museum London: https://artsandculture.google.com/partner/natural-history-museum

Nicholson, D. (2019) *Datalogging in Primary Science: A Quick Starter Guide*: www.sciencefix.co.uk/2019/10/datalogging-in-primary-science-a-quick-starter-guide/

Nicholson, D. (2021) *Creative Tools for Digital Storytelling in Class*: www.whiteboardblog.co.uk/2021/10/creative-tools-for-digital-storytelling-in-the-classroom/

Nicholson, D. (2022) 'Using branching databases for classification keys in primary science': www.sciencefix.co.uk/2022/11/using-branching-databases-for-classification-keys-in-primary-science

Phet Simulations: https://phet.colorado.edu/

PhyPhox: https://phyphox.org/

Science Museum London: www.sciencemuseum.org.uk/virtual-tour-science-museum
Smithsonian Museum Tour: https://naturalhistory2.si.edu/vt3/NMNH/
Solar System Scope: www.solarsystemscope.com/
Storyboard That: www.storyboardthat.com/storyboard-creator
The Wildlife Trusts webcams: www.wildlifetrusts.org/webcams
ThingLink: www.thinglink.com/

CHAPTER 17

Inspiring Future Scientists

Introduction

Science is essential for understanding and shaping our world, as it informs and influences our decisions and actions on various issues, such as health, environment, technology and society.

Science offers a wide range of opportunities and pathways for those who are interested and motivated to pursue scientific fields and professions. Science also needs a diverse and talented workforce that can contribute to the advancement and innovation of science, and that can address the current and future challenges and opportunities of our world.

Therefore, it is important to prepare children for scientific careers, and to nurture their potential and interest in science from an early age. This chapter will discuss the importance and challenges of science education in primary schools, and the strategies and practices that can help to foster and encourage children's engagement and aspiration in science.

Children's attitudes towards science

The ASPIRES project (Archer et al., 2013, 2020) suggests that from an early age many students begin to feel that although science is important, it is not a subject for them. Primary school children are already forming opinions on the areas of the curriculum that they like and enjoy, and those that they find 'boring'.

A study of pupils by the Wellcome Trust (2019) found that the number of pupils who find science interesting and who think they are good at science diminishes over their time in KS2. By the time they reach secondary school and receive careers guidance, their minds are made up, and many of them are not aware of, and don't even consider, the vast array of jobs and careers that involve or depend on science.

Even if they do not go on to work in science, in their roles as parents, citizens and voters, everyone should be able to engage with the big science issues that affect all of society, such as climate change or vaccination.

Archer et al. (2020) in the Aspires 2 project, looked at young people's science and career aspirations aged 10–14 and found that gender issues are evident from a young age.

Girls are less likely than boys to aspire to science careers, even though a higher percentage of girls than boys rate science as their favourite subject. Once they reach the age of 12–13 years, the research found that 18 per cent of boys and 12 per cent of girls aspire to become scientists, compared to 64 per cent of girls who aspire to careers in the arts.

The 2018 study, 'Drawing the future', found that by the far the most popular career that children aspired to was to become a sportsman or sportswoman. Boys were found to be over four times more likely to want to become an engineer than girls. Interestingly, girls are twice as likely to want to be a doctor compared to boys, and four times more likely to want to become a vet (Chambers et al., 2018).

The importance of science in a changing world

The world needs scientists. The children we can inspire into studying science now are the ones who will be called upon to solve the problems of the future.

The United Nations 17 Sustainable Development Goals provide us with many reasons for developing a scientifically literate population. Many of these goals require science, engineering and medical solutions (Shallcross, 2019). Climate change is a major threat, bringing with it associated impacts on food and water security and supplies. Along with this, the need for sustainable cities and the requirement for humans to produce affordable and clean energy, and to consume and produce responsibly, makes it very clear that future generations will have to be science-literate.

Scientists and stereotypes

Have you ever searched the internet for an image of a scientist? If you haven't, try it now. Although this has improved recently, most images you see will nearly all be white men wearing a lab coat. The stereotype of the mad scientist is a hard one to break.

An often-used way of seeing how pupils perceive scientists is to ask them to draw one. It's very likely that they will mostly draw white men in lab coats and glasses. Some will be bald; others will have crazy hairstyles. Most will look like Einstein, or Doc from *Back to the Future*. Very few will draw a female or a Black scientist, although this proportion has been increasing in recent years (Miller et al., 2018) largely due to the work done in schools.

This bias in the concept of what a scientist looks like even extends to the new AI image generation tools. I asked AI to draw a scientist (Adobe Firefly) and the results were mainly full of white men in lab coats.

This very white, very male image of science makes it hard to promote science as something for everyone. Many pupils don't envisage themselves becoming scientists as they don't see scientists who look like them.

Teachers have a responsibility to challenge these stereotypes and present a more diverse image of science. Pupils should feel that a career in science is something that is open to them, whatever their social group or gender. Not all science involves white coats – there are many scientists working in rainforests, deserts and even underwater.

Introduce the pupils to scientists such as Ibn al-Haytham, Sarah Gilbert, Marie Curie, George Washington Carver and Stephanie Kvolek to name just a few. There are many great examples of inspiring female scientists in the media such as Professor Alice Roberts, Dr Helen Czerski, Dr Maggie Aderin-Pocock, and more.

Teaching about scientists works best when they are closely related to the content that pupils are learning about at the time (Ofsted, 2023). Rather than spend time researching the scientists' lives, there should be a far greater focus on their work (Sinclair and Strachan, 2016). This emphasis provides children with the opportunity to think about the variety of enquiry types that have been used. You could also look at contemporary scientists alongside famous scientists from history to see how their work is related (Sinclair and Strachan, 2018).

Science capital

One of the key concepts that can help to understand and improve children's engagement and aspiration in science is **science capital,** a term that refers to the cultural, social and personal resources that influence people's relationship with science (Archer et al., 2015).

Science capital can include the following.

- Cultural resources, such as scientific knowledge, vocabulary and values.
- Social resources, such as family background, exposure to science-related activities and contacts with scientists or science professionals.
- Personal resources, such as interest, attitude and identity in relation to science.

Science capital can affect how children perceive and participate in science, and how they see themselves and their future in science.

Science capital incorporates an individual's attitudes and way of thinking. It can be useful to think of science capital as a bag you carry throughout life that contains all your science-related knowledge (what you know), attitudes (what you think), experiences (what you do) and contacts (who you know) (Godec et al., 2017).

It is important to increase children's science capital, and to provide them with various sources and forms of science capital. Some of the main sources and forms of science capital are:

Science at home The family background and environment of children can have a significant impact on their science capital, as they can provide them with exposure and access to science-related activities, such as watching science shows, visiting science museums or doing science experiments.

School environment The school environment can also play a vital role in enhancing children's science capital, as it can provide them with a science-rich atmosphere that can stimulate and sustain their curiosity and engagement in science. This includes science clubs and trips, as well as the curriculum.

Role models and mentors The people the children encounter and interact with who can inspire and influence them in their relationship with science. Role models and mentors can include various people, such as scientists or science professionals, who can showcase the diversity and excitement of science careers, and who can share their stories and experiences in science.

Increasing science capital

The Primary Science Capital Teaching Approach (Nag Chowdhuri et al., 2021) outlines three supporting pillars of practice.

1. **Personalising and localising**

This involves making science relevant to the everyday lives of the children in your class.

2. **Eliciting, valuing, linking and extending**

    Eliciting Bringing out children's personal, family and/or cultural experiences and knowledge within learning. Eliciting must be meaningful and must recognise students' lives and identities without being stereotypical or tokenistic.

    Valuing Explicitly recognising and acknowledging how these experiences and knowledge are relevant and enriching for everyone's learning.

    Linking Connecting students' contributions and experiences to appropriate aspects of the science curriculum.

    Extending Finding avenues beyond the lesson – within the school, community or across different lessons – to build children's contributions into wider teaching and learning.

3. **Building science capital**

To help support children's engagement with science, teachers can build their students' science capital by embedding the four areas of science capital across and throughout their lessons. The four areas are:

    What you know Understand science concepts, ideas and how science works.

    Who you know Recognise science skills that exist in their community. Connect children with people who use science in their jobs.

    How you think Develop their science-related attitudes to see science as everywhere and relevant.

    What you do Introduce children to relevant science media. Take part in science learning opportunities. Do science outside school.

                    (From Godec et al., 2017; Nag Chowdhuri et al., 2021)

Using science in the news

Using science-related news stories can help bridge the gap between the classroom and the 'real' world. Big news stories can be used to amaze or enthral the children, and hopefully inspire some to want to be scientists themselves.

News videos could be played and discussed as a class. News stories could be printed out and questions added for the children to answer as comprehension activities.

Emphasise the scientists behind the story, particularly if they can help break the stereotypical image of a scientist.

Use the news story as a springboard for other work. News articles could be used as story starters for extended pieces of writing or even poems. Children could rewrite the story for their own news reports and record them as short films or podcasts.

Connecting children with real scientists

A good way to inspire children is to get them into contact with real scientists. Websites such as STEM Directory and STEM Ambassadors support primary schools across the UK by helping young people and their teachers make links with STEM professionals in their area. Organisations like Stemettes and ScienceGrrl can provide female scientists to come into schools and run science events with a group of girls.

STEM Clubs

STEM Clubs are out-of-timetable sessions that enrich and broaden the curriculum, giving young people the chance to explore subjects like science, technology, engineering and maths in less formal settings.

Websites such as STEM Learning and My Science Club provide resources to help run an after-school club. You might even like to have your science club work towards awards such as the Crest Awards.

Further reading and resources

STEM support

British Science Week: www.britishscienceweek.org/
CREST Awards: www.crestawards.org/
Great Science Share for Schools: www.greatscienceshare.org/

I'm a Scientist, Get me out of here!: http://imascientist.org.uk/
My Science Club: www.myscienceclub.com/
Science Grrl: https://sciencegrrl.co.uk/
SoapboxScience: http://soapboxscience.org/
STEM Ambassadors: www.stem.org.uk/stem-ambassadors
STEM Club Activity Sets: www.stem.org.uk/primary/enrichment/stem-clubs/activities
STEM Directory: www.stem.org.uk/enrichment/stem-directory
STEMettes: http://stemettes.org/sis
STEM Women: www.stemwomen.com/

News sites for kids

BBC Newsround: www.bbc.co.uk/newsround/
Scholastic News: https://scholasticnews.scholastic.com/
Time for Kids: www.timeforkids.com
Twig Science Reporter: www.twigsciencereporter.com/
Twinkl News Room: www.twinkl.co.uk/newsroom

Subject associations

Association for Science Education: www.ase.org.uk
The British Science Association: www.britishscienceassociation.org/
The Institute of Engineering and Technology: www.theiet.org/
Institute of Physics (IoP): www.iop.org/
The Royal Institution: www.rigb.org
The Royal Society: www.royalsociety.org
The Royal Society of Biology: www.societyofbiology.org/
The Royal Society of Chemistry (RSC): www.rsc.org/

CHAPTER 18

Health and Safety in the Science Classroom

Introduction

Practical work is at the heart of science learning, yet there is a popular misconception that many practical activities in science can't be carried out in schools because of the limitations imposed by health and safety legislation (ASE, 2010). Managing health and safety in the classroom need not be difficult, nor should it inhibit effective and exciting science teaching.

When planning any science activity, the teacher should ensure that children are safe at all times. Any activity should be risk assessed when planning the lesson, and any potential problems identified and minimised.

Check with your school leadership team for the latest health and safety policies and guidance. It's their job to make sure that you and your colleagues have access to appropriate safety advice and, where necessary, training in order to work safely and effectively with children (Harding, 2021).

Hazards and risks

An important aspect of managing health and safety is making sure that all the relevant hazards are identified, the risks assessed and, if necessary, controlled and any 'significant findings' suitably recorded on the lesson plan (Borrows, 2003).

A **hazard** is anything that might cause harm ASE (2010). For example:

- Electricity at high voltages can kill.
- Some chemicals can burn the skin.
- Some microbes can make you sick.
- Some plants may cause allergic reactions.

A **risk** is the likelihood that a hazard will cause harm. This will depend on the chances of something going wrong in the lesson, how serious the injury would be and the number of people who might be affected ASE (2010).

Control measures are put in place to reduce the risk, but the hazard will still be present. The aim of the risk assessment is to reduce the risks to as low a level as reasonably practicable.

Nothing in life is completely safe and children should be introduced to the ideas of hazards and risks, and how to reduce them in their daily lives (ASE, 2010).

Sources of support

CLEAPSS

CLEAPSS is the only organisation in England, Wales and Northern Ireland that specialises in providing bespoke advice about keeping children safe during practical science, which is why most schools are already members. As membership is organised by your employer, it is quite common to find that your school is already a member but that no one knows about it. Contact CLEAPSS and they will be able to tell you.

If your school isn't a member, your employer (school, trust, local authority, etc.) must provide you and your colleagues with alternative, appropriate risk-assessment resources and advice (Harding, 2021).

In most cases, information about hazards and the safety measures you need to implement to reduce the risks during an activity can be found by searching the CLEAPSS website. If you can't find the information on their website, there is a helpline you can call.

Note

Schools in Scotland should use SSERC as an alternative source of support.

ASE *Be Safe*

Be Safe is a booklet produced by the ASE which gives additional guidance on health and safety matters for primary schools. It covers most of the science-based activities that will be found in the primary classroom. It could be used alongside CLEAPSS advice.

The risk-assessment process

Risk assessments are a key tool for ensuring health and safety in science. They are a systematic process of identifying, evaluating and controlling the risks that may arise, and of deciding whether the activity is safe and suitable to carry out.

Risk assessments help teachers to plan and deliver science lessons that are engaging and challenging, but also safe and appropriate for their pupils.

At the basic level the teacher should consider: 'I need to teach my children "X", using "Y" activity. What is the safest way to do this? What do I need to do for this to happen?' (CLEAPSS, 2021).

When you are planning the lesson, and you have decided on an activity to do, carry out these four steps as suggested by CLEAPSS (2021):

- **Read** Use the CLEAPSS website to see what it says about how to do the activity safely.
- **Think** Think about how you will implement the safety measures CLEAPSS has recommended, so that they will work for your class.
- **Record** Make a note of the safety measures somewhere useful, so that you remember to carry them out. Typically, this can go at the end of your lesson plan, but it could go in your teacher planner.
- **Do** Carry out the activity and make sure the safety measures you have planned are implemented.

Things to consider when planning a practical task

Do you have children with particular educational needs that may need additional support to carry out the activity safely? Will you have an additional adult?

Do you need to split the class and have a small group doing the activity while the rest of the class are doing independent work?

Plan how you will support the children to use specific pieces of equipment and handle materials – for example, modelling how to use it and how to behave while using it.

How will you get the equipment to the children and back again? Often it could be placed on each table in trays. However, sometimes you may have to plan how the children are going to collect and return some equipment or resources from another part of the classroom.

What procedures do you have for counting out and counting in certain items, such as scissors?

If you think the children are in a troublesome mood – for example, a high-risk activity would normally take place straight after lunch on a Friday afternoon – consider rescheduling it to another time.

When recording the safety measures needed, do you need to make a sign to go next to a piece of equipment to warn of the risk? Should you add additional messages to your PowerPoint or any instruction sheet the children are following?

Safety equipment

Primary science is very different to secondary school science. It typically takes place in a classroom, rather than a laboratory, the teacher is a non-specialist and there is no science technician support. This will limit the range of practical activities you can do, particularly with chemicals. If your risk assessment requires personal protective equipment (PPE) in any form – for example, eye protection or safety gloves – then the general guidance is that the activity is probably not suitable for you to carry out in your classroom (CLEAPSS, 2021).

This does not count for clothing that might protect from getting dirty, such as aprons when doing something messy or gloves when gardening. Keep using those if you need to.

Further reading and resources

ASE *Be safe*!: www.millgatehouse.co.uk/product/be-safe/
CLEAPSS: https://primary.cleapss.org.uk/
Health and Safety Executive: www.hse.gov.uk/education/
SSERC: www.sserc.org.uk/

References

AKSIS Project (2004) 'ASE King's College London Science Investigations in Schools'. Available at: www.kcl.ac.uk/archive/website-resources/education/web-files2/aksis.pdf

Allen, M. (2019) *Misconceptions in Primary Science*. Maidenhead: Open University Press.

Andersson, J., Löfgren, R. and Tibell, L. (2020) 'What's in the body? Children's annotated drawings', *Journal of Biological Education*, 54 (2): 176–90. Available at: www.tandfonline.com/doi/full/10.1080/00219266.2019.1569082

Archer Ker, L., DeWitt, J., Osborne, J.F., Dillon, J.S., Wong, B. and Willis, B. (2013) 'ASPIRES Report: Young people's science and career aspirations, age 10–14'. King's College London Research Portal. Available at: https://kclpure.kcl.ac.uk/ws/portalfiles/portal/64130521/ASPIRES_Report_2013.pdf

Archer, L., Dawson, E., DeWitt, J., Seakins, A. and Wong, B. (2015) '"Science capital": a conceptual, methodological, and empirical argument for extending bourdieusian notions of capital beyond the arts', *Journal of Research in Science Teaching*, 52 (7): 922–48. Available at: www.researchgate.net/publication/273789179_Science_capital_A_conceptual_methodological_and_empirical_argument_for_extending_bourdieusian_notions_of_capital_beyond_the_arts_SCIENCE_CAPITAL

Archer, L., Moote, J., MacLeod, E., Francis, B. and DeWitt, J. (2020) 'ASPIRES 2: Young people's science and career aspirations, age 10–19'. London: UCL Institute of Education. Available at: https://discovery.ucl.ac.uk/id/eprint/10092041/15/Moote_9538%20UCL%20Aspires%202%20report%20full%20online%20version.pdf

Asoko, H. (1995) 'Faulty connections'. Available at: www.tes.com/news/faulty-connections

Asoko, H. (2002) 'Developing conceptual understanding in primary science', *Cambridge Journal of Education*, 32 (2): 153–64. DOI: 10.1080/03057640220147522

Asoko, H. and De Boo, M. (2001) *Analogies and Illustrations: Representing Ideas in Primary Science*. Hatfield: Association for Science Education.

Association for Science Education (ASE) (2010) *Be Safe! Health and Safety in School Science and Technology for Teachers of 3- to 12-year-olds*. Association for Science Education. Hatfield (ase.org.uk).

Association for Science Education (ASE) (2018) 'Scientific enquiry in the UK'. Available at: www.ase.org.uk/system/files/Scientific%20Enquiry%20in%20 the%20UK%20V2.pdf

Bennett, J., Dunlop, L., Atkinson, L., Compton, S., Glasspoole-Bird, H., Lubben, F., Reiss, M.J. and Turkenburg-van Diepen, M. (2023) 'A systematic review of approaches to primary science teaching'. London: Education Endowment Foundation. Available at: https://educationendowmentfoundation.org.uk/education-evidence/ evidence-reviews/primary-science

Bianchi, L., Whittaker, A. and Poole, A. (2021) *The 10 Key Issues with Children's Learning in Primary Science in England*. University of Manchester and The Ogden Trust. Available at: www.scienceacrossthecity.co.uk/wpcontent/ uploads/2021/03/3634_Childrens_Learning_in_Primary_Science_ Report_2020_v8.pdf

Black, P. and William, D. (2010) 'Inside the black box raising standards through classroom assessment'. Available at: www.researchgate.net/ publication/44836144_Inside_the_Black_Box_Raising_Standards_ Through_Classroom_Assessment

Bloom, B.S. (1956) *Taxonomy of Educational Objectives: The Classification of Educational Goals; Handbook I: Cognitive Domain*. London: Longman.

Bolton, N. (2020) 'Grab a bucket, we're taking science outdoors', *Primary Science*, 161: 33–5. Available at: www.ase.org.uk/resources/primary-science/issue-161

Borrows, P. (2003) 'Managing health and safety in primary science', *Primary Science Review*, 79: 18–20, September–October.

Caravita, S. and Falchetti, E. (2005) 'Are bones alive?', *Journal of Biological Education*, 39 (4): 163–70. Available at: www.tandfonline.com/doi/abs/10.10 80/00219266.2005.9655990

Carle, E. (1969) *The Very Hungry Caterpillar*. London: Puffin.

Caviglioli, O. (2019) *Dual Coding with Teachers*. Melton: John Catt Publishing.

Centre for the Use of Research and Evidence in Education (CUREE) (2011) 'Effective classroom talk in science'. Available at: www.curee.co.uk/node/4836

Chambers, N., Kashefpakdel, E., Rehill, J. and Percy, C. (2018) 'Drawing the future: exploring the career aspirations of primary school children from around the world'. Available at: www.educationandemployers.org/wp-content/uploads/2018/01/DrawingTheFuture.pdf

Chapman, S. (2014) 'Teaching the "big ideas" of electricity at primary level', *Primary Science*, 135. Available at: www.ase.org.uk/resources/primary-science/issue-135/teaching-thebig-ideas-electricity-primary-level

Chin, C. (2007) 'Teacher questioning in science classrooms: approaches that stimulate productive thinking', *Journal of Research in Science Teaching*, 44 (6): 815–43. Available at: www.stem.org.uk/system/files/community-resources/legacy_files_migrated/10174-Chin-2007-Journal_of_Research_in_Science_Teaching.pdf

Chiu, M.-H. and Lin, J.-W. (2005) 'Promoting fourth graders' conceptual change of their understanding of electric current via multiple analogies', *Journal of Research in Science Teaching*, 42 (4): 429–64. Available at: www.researchgate.net/publication/227658723 Promoting_fourth_graders%27_conceptual_change_of_their_understanding_of_electric_current_via_multiple_analogies

Christidou, V., Kazela, K., Kakana, D. and Valakosta, M. (2009) 'Teaching magnetic attraction to preschool children: a comparison of different approaches', *International Journal of Learning*, 16: 115–28. Available at: www.researchgate.net/publication/286096686_Teaching_magnetic_attraction_to_preschool_children_A_comparison_of_different_approaches

Churchill, N. and Barratt-Pugh, C. (2020) 'The digital entanglement of humanities, literacy, and storytelling'. In K.W.S. Kung (ed.), *Reconceptualizing the Digital Humanities in Asia*. Singapore: Springer Nature. pp. 141–54. Available at: https://link.springer.com/chapter/10.1007%2F978-981-15-4642-6_9

CLEAPSS (2021) 'How to do a risk assessment'. Available at: https://primary.cleapss.org.uk/Resource-File/P137-How-to-do-a-risk-assessment.pdf

Department for Education (DfE) (2008) National Strategies: 'Understanding misconceptions'. Available at: www.stem.org.uk/resources/elibrary/resource/31725/understanding-misconceptions

Department for Education (DfE) (2013a) 'National curriculum in England: science programmes of study'. Available at: www.gov.uk/government/publications/national-curriculum-in-england-science-programmes-of-study/national-curriculum-in-england-science-programmes-of-study

Department for Education (DfE) (2013b) 'National curriculum in England: computing programmes of study'. Available at: www.gov.uk/government/publications/national-curriculum-in-england-computing-programmes-of-study

Department for Education (DfE) (2023) 'Key Stage 2 attainment, academic year 2022/23'. Available at: https://explore-education-statistics.service.gov.uk/find-statistics/key-stage-2-attainment

Dillon, J. and Lovell, B. (2022) 'Links between natural environments, learning and health: evidence briefing'. Available at: https://publications.naturalengland.org.uk/publication/5745607154335744

Dillon, J., Morris, M., O'Donnell, L., Reid, A., Rikinson, M. and Scott, W. (2005) 'Engaging and learning with the outdoors: the final report of the outdoor classroom in a rural context action research project'. Slough: National Foundation for Educational Research.

Donaldson, J. (1999) *The Gruffalo*. London: Macmillan.

Durran, J. (2021) 'Key learning questions: an introduction'. Available at: https://jamesdurran.blog/2021/08/28/key-learning-questions-an-introduction/

Education Endowment Foundation (EEF) (2021) 'Cognitive science approaches in the classroom'. Available at: https://educationendowmentfoundation.org.uk/education-evidence/evidence-reviews/cognitive-science-approaches-in-the-classroom

Education Endowment Foundation (EEF) (2023) 'Improving primary science guidance report'. Available at: https://educationendowmentfoundation.org.uk/education-evidence/guidance-reports/primary-science-ks1-ks2

Education Policy Institute (EPI) (2023) 'Annual report on the state of education in England'. Available at: https://epi.org.uk/publications-and-research/annual-report-2023/

Forsey, K. (2014) 'Taking the new curriculum outdoors', *Primary Science*, 132: 9–11. Available at: www.ase.org.uk/resources/primary-science/issue-132

Foster, C. (2012) 'Creationism as a misconception: socio-cognitive conflict in the teaching of evolution', *International Journal of Science Education*, 34 (14): 2171–80. DOI: 10.1080/09500693.2012.692102

Godec, S., King, H. and Archer, L. (2017) *The Science Capital Teaching Approach: Engaging Students with Science, Promoting Social Justice*. London: University College London. Available at: https://discovery.ucl.ac.uk/id/eprint/10080166/1/the-science-capital-teaching-approach-pack-for-teachers.pdf

Grimshaw, M., Curwen, L., Morgan, J., Shallcross, N., Franklin, S. and Shallcross, D. (2019) 'The benefits of outdoor learning on science teaching', *Journal of Emergent Science,* 19: 40–5. Available at: www.ase.org.uk/system/files/Grimshaw%20et%20al_0.pdf

Harding, J. (2021) 'Health and safety', from *Primary Science Leader's Survival Guide 2021 Edition*. Available at: www.ase.org.uk/resources/primary-science-leaders-survival-guide-2021-edition

Harlen, W. (ed.) (2010) *Principles and Big Ideas of Science Education*. Hatfield: ASE. Available at: www.ase.org.uk/bigideas

Harlen, W. and Qualter, A. (2018) *The Teaching of Science in Primary Schools*. Meadville, PA: David Fulton Publishers.

Harris, M.A. (2023) 'Growing among trees: a 12-month process evaluation of school based outdoor learning interventions', *Journal of Adventure Education and Outdoor Learning*, 23 (3): 232–43. DOI: 10.1080/14729679.2021.2001758

Higgins, S., Xiao, Z. and Katsipataki. M. (2012) *The Impact of Digital Technology on Learning: A Summary. Education Endowment Foundation*. Available at: https://educationendowmentfoundation.org.uk/education-evidence/evidence-reviews/digital-technology-2012

Hoath, L. and Dave, H. (2022) *Sustainability and Climate Change Education: Creating the Foundations for Effective Improvement*. Leeds Trinity University and the Teacher Development Trust. Available at: https://tdtrust.org/2022/07/11/sustainability-and-climate-education-creating-the-foundations-for-effective-improvement-report/

Hodgson, C. (2010) *Assessment for Learning in Primary Science: Practices and Benefits. National Foundation for Educational Research*. Available at: www.nfer.ac.uk/publications/AAS02/AAS02.pdf

Holman, J. (2017) *Good Practical Science*. London: Gatsby Foundation. Available at: www.gatsby.org.uk/education/programmes/support-for-practical-science-in-schools

Holzwarth, W. (2019) *The Story of the Little Mole Who Knew it Was None of his Business*. London: Pavilion.

Horlock, J., Naylor, S. and Moules, J. (2015) *Let's Talk About Evolution*. Hatfield: Millgate House.

Jones, K. (2019) *Retrieval Practice: Research and Resources for Every Classroom*. Melton: John Catt.

Jones, K. (2022) *Retrieval Practice: Primary. A Guide for Primary Teachers and Leaders*. Melton: John Catt.

Kara, Y. and Yesilyurt, S. (2007) 'Comparing the impacts of tutorial and edutainment software programs on students' achievements, misconceptions, and attitudes towards biology', *Journal of Science Education and Technology*, 17 (1): 32–41.

Kibble, B. (2002) 'How do you picture electricity?', *Primary Science Review*, 74: 28–30.

Leahy, S., Lyon, C., Thompson, M. and Wiliam, D. (2005) 'Classroom assessment: minute by minute, day by day', *Educational Leadership*, 63 (3): 18–24. Available at: www.researchgate.net/publication/237795503_Classroom_Assessment_Minute_by_Minute_Day_by_Day_In_classrooms_that_use_assessment_to_support_learning_teachers_continually_adapt_instruction_to_meet_student_needs

Lee, K.-W. and Tan, S.-N. (2004) 'Atoms and molecules: do they have a place in primary science?', *Primary Science Review*, 82: 21–3.

Leinhardt, G. (1992) 'What research on learning tells us about teaching', *Educational Leadership*, 49: 20–5.

Limón, M. (2001) 'On the cognitive conflict as an instructional strategy for conceptual change: a critical appraisal', *Learning and Instruction*, 11 (4–5): 357–80. Available at: https://doi.org/10.1016/S0959-4752(00)00037-2.

Malone, K. (2008) '"Every experience matters". An evidence-based research report on the role of learning outside the classroom for children's whole development from birth to eighteen years'. Report commissioned by Farming and Countryside Education for UK, Department of Children, School and Families, Wollongong, Australia.

Massie, J. and Long, J. (2009) MET: 'Simulation for science education'. Available at: https://wiki.ubc.ca/MET:Simulation_for_Science_Education

McCrory, A. (2017) 'Scientific enquiry and engaging primary-aged children in science lessons – Part 2. Why teach science via enquiry?', *Journal of Emergent Science*, 14: 28–39. Available at: www.ase.org.uk/resources/journal-of-emergent-science/issue-14

McMahon, K., McKay, D. and Lee, A. (2021) 'The learning sciences and primary school science'. Bath Space University/Wellcome. Available at: https://research-space.bathspa.ac.uk/13965/

Mercer, N., Dawes, L. and Kleine Starrman, J. (2009) 'Dialogic teaching in the primary science classroom', *Language and Education Journal*, 23: (4).

Miller, D., Nolla, D., Eagly, A. and Uttal, D. (2018) 'The development of children's gender-science stereotypes: a meta-analysis of 5 decades of U.S. draw-a-scientist studies', *Child Development*, 89 (6): 1943–55. Available at: https://srcd.onlinelibrary.wiley.com/doi/full/10.1111/cdev.13039

Minchin, T. (2009) 'Storm'. © Navel Enterprises. Available at: https://youtu.be/jIWj3tl-DXg

Nag Chowdhuri, M., King, H. and Archer, L. (2021) *The Primary Science Capital Teaching Approach: Teacher Handbook*. London: University College London. Available at: www.ucl.ac.uk/ioe/departments-and-centres/departments/education-practice-and-society/stem-participation-social-justice-research/primary-science-capital-project

Natural Connections (2016) *Transforming Outdoor Learning in Schools: Lessons from the Natural Connections Project*. Available at: www.plymouth.ac.uk/uploads/production/document/path/7/7634/Transforming_Outdoor_Learning_in_Schools_SCN.pdf

Naylor, S. (2015) 'Talking and thinking using concept cartoons: what have we learnt?', *School Science Review*, 97: 61–7. Available at: www.ase.org.uk/system/files/SSR%20December%202015%20061-067%20Naylor.pdf

Nicholson, D. (2011) 'Using a visualiser in primary science', *Primary Science*, 118: 23–5.

Nicholson, D. (2019) 'Data logging in primary science: a quick starter guide'. Available at: www.sciencefix.co.uk/2019/10/datalogging-in-primary-science-a-quick-starter-guide/

Ofsted (2008) *Learning Outside the Classroom*. Available at: https://ltl.org.uk/wp-content/uploads/2020/05/ofsted-learning-outside-the-classroom.pdf

Ofsted (2013) 'Maintaining curiosity: a survey into science education in schools'. Available at: www.gov.uk/government/publications/maintaining-curiosity-a-survey-into-science-education-in-schools

Ofsted (2021) *Research Review Series: Science*. Available at: www.gov.uk/government/publications/research-review-series-science/research-review-series-science

Ofsted (2023) *Finding the Optimum: Science Subject Report*. Available at: www.gov.uk/government/publications/subject-report-series-science/finding-the-optimum-the-science-subject-report–2

OPAL (Open Air Laboratories) (2015) 'Citizen science for everyone: soil and earthworm survey'. Imperial College London. Available at: www.imperial.ac.uk/opal/surveys/soilsurvey/

Osbourne, J., Wadsworth, P., Black, P. and Meadows, J. (1994) *SPACE Project Research Report: The Earth in Space*. Available at: www.stem.org.uk/elibrary/resource/29214

Patrick, P. and Tunnicliffe, S. (2011) 'What plants and animals do early childhood and primary students name? Where do they see them?' *Journal of Science Education and Technology*, 20: 630–42. DOI 10.1007/s10956-011-9290-7. Available at: www.researchgate.net/publication/225753261_What_Plants_and_Animals_Do_Early_Childhood_and_Primary_Students%27_Name_Where_Do_They_See_Them

Piaget J., trans. Tomlinson, J. and Tomlinson, A. (1929) *The Child's Conception of the World*. New York: Harcourt Brace.

Pine, K., Messer, D. and St John, K. (2001) 'Children's misconceptions in primary science: a survey of teachers' views', *Research in Science & Technological Education*, 19 (1): 7–9. Available at: https://doi.org/10.1080/02635140120046240

Podolefsky, N., Perkins, K. and Adams, W. (2010) 'Factors promoting engaged exploration with computer simulations', *Physical Review ST Physics Education*

Research, 6 (1). Available at: https://journals.aps.org/prper/abstract/10.1103/PhysRevSTPER.6.020117

Pottle, J. (2019) *The Molliebird: An Evolution Story.* Bristol: Primary Science Teaching Trust Trading. Available at: www.sciencethroughstory.com/the-molliebird

Ramos, M. (2011) 'Analogies as tools for making meaning in elementary science education. How do they work in classroom settings?', *Eurasia Journal of Mathematics, Science and Technology,* 7: 29–9. Available at: www.ejmste.com/download/analogies-as-tools-for-meaningmaking-in-elementary-scienceeducation-how-do-they-work-inclassroom-4201.pdf

Reiss, M. and Tunnicliffe, S. (2001) 'Students' understandings of human organs and organ systems', *Research in Science Education,* 31: 383–99. DOI 10.1023/A:1013116228261

Rosenshine, B. (2012) 'Principles of instruction: research-based strategies that all teachers should know', *American Educator,* 36 (1): 12–39.

Royal Society of Chemistry (RSC) (2015) 'Talk for primary science'. Available at: https://edu.rsc.org/primary-science/talk-for-primary-science/2104.article

Russell, T. and McGuigan, L. (2015) 'Animals don't just grow feathers when they want to . . . ', *Primary Science,* 138: 18–21.

Shallcross, D. (2019) 'Why does the teaching of science at primary school matter?', *Journal of Emergent Science,* 1: 3–5. Available at: www.ase.org.uk/system/files/journal-issue/documents/JES%2018%20Winter%202019-20%20revised.pdf

Sinclair, A. and Strachan, A. (2016) 'The messy nature of science: famous scientists can help clear up', *Primary Science,* 145: 21–3. Available at: www.ase.org.uk/resources/primary-science/issue-145/messy-nature-science-famous-scientists-can-help-clear

Sinclair, A. and Strachan, A. (2018) 'Standing on the shoulders of giants: contemporary scientists bringing your science curriculum to life', *Primary Science,* 151: 10–13. Available at: www.ase.org.uk/system/files/journal-issue/documents/Primary%20Science%20151_0.pdf

Skamp, K. (2005) 'Teaching about stuff', *Primary Science Review,* 89 (20–2).

Smallman, S. (2015) *Poo in the Zoo.* London: Little Tiger Press.

SPACE Project Research Report (1990a) 'Light'. Available at: www.stem.org.uk/resources/ elibrary/resource/29216/space-project-research-report-light

SPACE Project Research Report (1990b) 'Sound'. Available at: www.stem.org.uk/resources/ elibrary/resource/29213/space-project-research-report-sound

SPACE (Science Processes and Concepts Exploration project) (1993) 'Research reports: rocks, soils and weather', Liverpool University Press. Available at: www.stem.org.uk/rxwjv

Spring, H. (2021) *Teaching Primary Science Outdoors*. Hatfield: ASE/Millgate House.

STEM Learning (2016) 'National curriculum: Science'. Available at: www.stem.org.uk/resources/collection/3201/national-curriculum-science

Thomas, I. (2018) *Moth: An Evolution Story*. London: Bloomsbury. Available at: https://isabelthomas.co.uk/project/moth/

Tracy, C. (2014) 'Energy in the new curriculum: an opportunity for change', *School Science Review*, 96: 51–61.

Tucker, Z. (2019) *Greta and the Giants: Inspired by Greta Thunberg's Stand to Save the World*. London: Frances Lincoln.

Turner, J., Keogh, B., Naylor, S. and Lawrence, L. (2011) *It's Not Fair – Or Is It? A Guide to Developing Children's Ideas Through Primary Science Enquiry*. Hatfield: Millgate House.

Tytler, R., Peterson, S. and Prain, V. (2006) 'Picturing evaporation: learning science literacy through a particle representation', *Teaching Science* (Journal of the Australian Science Teachers Association), 52 (1): 12–17.

Varelas, M., Pappas, J., Kane, J. and Arsenault, M., Hankes, J. and Cowan, B.M. (2007) 'Urban primary-grade children think and talk science: curricular and instructional practices that nurture participation and argumentation', *Science Education*, 92 (1): 65–95. Available at: https://onlinelibrary.wiley.com/doi/10.1002/sce.20232

Wardell, R. (2022) 'Using cognitive science principles to design a knowledge-rich primary science curriculum'. Chartered College of Teaching. Available at: https://my.chartered.college/impact_article/using-cognitive-science-principles-to-design-a-knowledge-rich-primary-science-curriculum-2/

Wellcome (2014) 'Primary science: is it missing out?' Available at: https://cms.wellcome.org/sites/default/files/primary-science-is-it-missing-out-wellcome-sep14.pdf

Wellcome (2017) '"State of the nation" report of UK Primary Science Education. Available at: https://wellcome.org/reports/state-nation-report-uk-primary-science-education

Wellcome (2019) *What Pupils Think of Science in Primary Schools*. Available at: https://cms.wellcome.org/sites/default/files/what-pupils-think-of-science-in-primary-schools.pdf

Wellcome (2021) 'Primary science education beyond 2021 – what next?' Available at: www.stem.org.uk/system/files/elibrary-resources/2021/11/Primary%20science%20after%202021_0.pdf

Williams, J. (2014) 'Evolution versus creationism: a matter of acceptance versus belief', *Journal of Biological Education*. Available at: www.tandfonline.com/doi/full/10.1080/00219266.2014.943790

Index

Page numbers followed by "f" indicate figures; those followed by "t" indicate tables.